FALLIBLE

PROPHETS

OF NEW CALVINISM

An Analysis, Critique, and Exhortation Concerning

the Contemporary Doctrine of

"Fallible Prophecy"

MICHAEL JOHN BEASLEY

THE

FALLIBLE
PROPHETS
OF NEW CALVINISM

An Analysis, Critique, and Exhortation Concerning

the Contemporary Doctrine of

"Fallible Prophecy"

Published by:

The
Armoury
Ministries

www.thearmouryministries.org

Dedication

To my children who are precious

gifts from the Lord. May the

Lord sanctify you in truth -

His Word is truth.

John 17:17

The Fallible Prophets of New Calvinism: An Analysis, Critique, and Exhortation Concerning the Contemporary Doctrine of "Fallible Prophecy"
ISBN: 978-1-935358-13-8
Copyright © 2013 by Michael John Beasley.

Library of Congress Cataloging-in-Publication Data
Michael John Beasley
The Fallible Prophets of New Calvinism: An Analysis, Critique, and Exhortation Concerning the Contemporary Doctrine of "Fallible Prophecy"
  Includes bibliographic references and index
  Library of Congress Registration Claim: C-1-1003260971
  10/01/2013

Illustration by Gerard Hoet (1648-1733) (detail). Image courtesy of Bizzell Bible Collection, University of Oklahoma Libraries.

For more information go to www.thearmouryministries.org

Isaiah 55:8–11:

8 "For My thoughts are not your thoughts, Nor are your ways

My ways," declares the LORD. 9 "For as the heavens are higher than the

earth, So are My ways higher than your ways And My thoughts than your

thoughts. 10 "For as the rain and the snow come down from heaven, and

do not return there without watering the earth and making it bear and

sprout, And furnishing seed to the sower and bread to the eater;

11 So will My word be which goes forth from My mouth;

It will not return to Me empty,

Without accomplishing what I desire,

And without succeeding in the matter

for which I sent it."

Table of Contents

INTRODUCTION:

A PRIMER ON

PROPHECY

The fact that you have taken this work in hand signifies that you have some form of interest in the subject of *fallible prophecy*.[1] What I cannot know is the particular perspective you already have as you come to this book. Perhaps you are deeply studied on this matter, or you are just wondering what this is all about. Perhaps you are convinced that *fallible prophecy* is right, wrong, positive, or negative – I do not know. What I do know is that any subject dealing with spiritual gifts is neither small nor trivial. Because of this, I would like to begin with an important *context* and *personal confession*. The context that I wish to offer the reader has to do with the church's *valuation of spiritual gifts*. When it comes to the valuation of spiritual gifts, the great danger for any generation is to swing the pendulum of emphasis too far in either direction thereby *overemphasizing* or *underemphasizing* Christ's gifts to the church. The gifts and provisions that Christ has sacrificially given to the church for her maturation should be cherished, not ignored; appreciated, but not worshipped.[2] A careful study of Ephesians 4 reminds us that the church's charge to *preserve the unity of the Spirit in the bond of peace* is a very serious one; one that is impossible without the *sacrificial gifts and provisions of Christ our Savior*. I say sacrificial gifts in light of Paul's description of the Savior who *descended and ascended* in order to *give gifts to men* (Ephesians 4:7-10). Paul goes on to describe the substance and purpose of Christ's gifts as follows:

> Ephesians 4:11–16: 11 And He gave some as apostles, and some as prophets, and some as evangelists, and some as pastors and teachers, 12 for the equipping of the saints for the work of service, to the building up of the body of Christ; 13 until we all attain to the unity of the faith, and of the knowledge of the Son of God, to a mature man, to the measure of the stature which belongs to the fullness of Christ. 14 As a result, we are no longer to be children, tossed

---

[1] Throughout this book, the words *fallible prophecy* will be in italics in order to distinguish it as an expression representing a very specific set of ideas and definitions that will be developed and explained within the pages of this book.

[2] Ephesians 4:1-6.

here and there by waves and carried about by every wind of doctrine, by the trickery of men, by craftiness in deceitful scheming; 15 but speaking the truth in love, we are to grow up in all aspects into Him who is the head, even Christ, 16 from whom the whole body, being fitted and held together by what every joint supplies, according to the proper working of each individual part, causes the growth of the body for the building up of itself in love.

Paul offers us two ways to measure the inestimable value of Christ's gifts: 1. They came by Christ's condescension, self-sacrifice, and victorious resurrection (Ephesians 4:7-10); and 2. Without such gifts, the church will most certainly be *carried about by every wind of doctrine* (Ephesians 4:11-16). Since the purpose of these gifts is to magnify Christ through the proclamation of His word, they are indispensable with respect to the church's spiritual purity and growth. Christ's gift of the Apostles, along with their attending signs, wonders, and divine revelation; the gift of His prophets in the Spirit who also disclosed God's divine revelation of the mystery of Christ (Ephesians 3:1-13); the gift of His evangelists who advance the message of the Gospel to the lost; His pastors and His teachers who rightly divide the Word of God for Christ's sheep – all of these provisions come from Christ for the maturation of the body so that His saints would not be like children tossed about by the trickery of men (Ephesians 4:14), but would become mature to the measure of the stature which belongs to the fullness of Christ (Ephesians 4:13). In everything, such gifts are given so that Christ's body would be collectively built up "in love." In view of these matters we should avoid the extreme of making light of these gifts, or deriding their nature and purpose. To do so would be to *dishonor to the One who sacrificed Himself in order to lavish such gifts upon the church.* Such an error is no small matter, the gravity of which is difficult to fathom – but we must seek to comprehend such matters as Christ continues to sanctify us all. In all of this, we should also consider another extreme approach to spiritual gifts, one that leads to their exaltation and over-valuation:

Luke 10:17–20: 17 The seventy returned with joy, saying, "Lord, even the demons are subject to us in Your name." 18 And He said to them, "I was watching Satan fall from heaven like lightning. 19 "Behold, I have given you authority to tread on serpents and scorpions, and over all the power of the enemy, and nothing will injure you. 20 "Nevertheless do not rejoice in this, that the spirits are subject to you, but rejoice that your names are recorded in heaven."

This portion of Luke 10 reveals the disciples' response to their brief missionary journey (Luke 10:1-16). Remarkably, the disciples' joy and exuberance was not reciprocated by the Savior. Rather than joining in their celebration that *even the demons were subject to them in Christ's name,* Jesus corrects their focus entirely by instructing them *to rejoice because their names are recorded in heaven.* We must not underestimate the gravity and importance of the Savior's teaching, after all, a soul that is not centrally focused on Christ and His kingdom is a soul that is fully deceived, as Jesus also said:

Matthew 7:22–23: 22 "Many will say to Me on that day, 'Lord, Lord, did we not prophesy in Your name, and in Your name cast out demons, and in Your name perform many miracles?' 23 "And then I will declare to them, 'I never knew you; Depart from Me, you who practice lawlessness.'"

When we consider the collective message of these passages, we are reminded that the difference between focusing on the *God of our salvation* versus *the temporal gifts that He bestows* is the approximate difference between *heaven and hell.* Yes, we are to rejoice that Christ has given gifts to His church for the building up of the body, but this must never constitute our chief joy above all (Luke 10:20). Above everything else, Christ and His eternal kingdom must be the ultimate wellspring of our joy, and the spiritual gifts that He gives must take their proper place lest we enter into the realm of self-deception and self-exaltation. I would submit to the reader that these principles are not small or insignificant;

instead they are deeply important and offer us a crucial *context* for the remainder of our study.

As for my *confession*, I must say that I feel a profound sense of frailty in writing this book. It is partly my sense of fatigue that comes in producing a polemical work, but it is mostly my sense of awe over the great subject at hand. I cannot possibly express my sense of gratitude and amazement for the Lord's gift of the Holy Spirit. From the miracle of my regeneration to the present day, I feel utterly overwhelmed by the comfort and joy that can only come through the Spirit's patient, sanctifying work in my life. Without Him I would never be pierced through with conviction over my own sin;[3] without Him the Scriptures would have continued to appear as utter foolishness to my corrupted mind;[4] without His precious intercession on my behalf my cries to God would be utter futility;[5] as a pastor I would never have any hope of others being illumined, convicted, and encouraged by the preached word;[6] without Him my marriage and family would be a fruitless disaster,[7] I would remain dead in my trespasses and sins,[8] and I would never have any hope to share the Gospel with others[9] nor would I have the desire or the perseverance to endure all things for the sake of those who are chosen.[10]

Without the Spirit; without the Son; without the Father – I would be nothing.

---

[3] Psalm 51.

[4] 1 Corinthians 1:18a.

[5] Romans 8:15.

[6] 1 Corinthians 1:18b.

[7] Ephesians 5:18-6:4.

[8] John 3:1-8.

[9] Romans 1:16.

[10] 2 Timothy 2:10.

Therefore, I joyfully begin with this *confession* of mine, for it seems necessary in light of the discussion of spiritual gifts. I would ask the reader to consider the contents of this book in view of this author's debt of gratitude for the one who is called "another Helper."[11] In light of this, I feel a great sense of trepidation as I write, seeing that the gifts and workings of the Holy Spirit are of much greater value and weight than either you or I could fully comprehend in this life. Yet I write as one who desires to see what it is that the Holy Spirit has revealed in His word concerning the subject of spiritual gifts. Though there are many important subjects that we could address within such a broad topic, the particular focus of our study will pertain to that of the proposed doctrine of *fallible prophecy*. One of the great challenges I have found with this subject of *fallible prophecy* is that it contains a great number of conflicts and unresolved questions. Thus, if all possible questions were pursued with great force, this book would become an extensive tome. However, my goal is not to write a tome but to simplify core concerns which surround the doctrine of *fallible prophecy* in order to equip the reader with some helpful, scriptural discernment. To begin our study let us establish some basic matters of thought concerning our subject at hand. Very simply, many *continuationists* believe that the prophetic gifts, given to the early church, are *continuing* in the present day and that among them...

"... there are those who hold that these gifts are *fallible* in their exercise and have an authority lower than that of the Old Testament canonical prophets and the New Testament apostles."[12]

---

[11] The Spirit is called *another* Helper [*paraklēton*] since "Jesus Christ the righteous" is referred to as our Advocate [*paraklēton*] with the Father – 1 John 2:1.

[12] Richard B. Gaffin Jr., Robert L. Saucy, C. Samuel Storms, Douglas A. Oss, <u>Are Miraculous Gifts for Today?</u>, ed. Wayne A. Grudem (Grand Rapids MI: Zondervan Publishing, 1996), 46 Italics mine.

Though the view of *continuationists* on the subject of prophecy can vary considerably, most hold to some form of *non-authoritative, fallible prophecy* for the modern church. What is so striking about this view is that its advocates insist that the New Testament prophet is both *fallible* and *legitimate* at the same time. Thus, when such a "prophet" speaks, an admixture of truth and error is delivered to the church, yet despite this, such a prophet is not regarded as false. Though such prophets claim to receive direct revelations from God, their spoken prophecies are often corrupted by their own "merely human words."[13] Though a more thorough argument will be developed throughout the pages of this book, I would like to address several reasons why such a notion of prophecy is problematic and even dangerous to the church in any age:

- The concepts presented within *fallible prophecy* do more than merely shift the meaning of prophecy from the standard of Old Testament revelation – *they completely reverse the meaning of prophecy altogether.* Within the system of *fallible prophecy* the modern prophet is not seen as *infallible,* but is now considered to be *fallible.* The lexical argument for this conclusion comes from *the most extreme uses of the secular Greek language* along with other *extrabiblical sources.* Thus, the advocates of *fallible prophecy* are arguing that the 1st century readers of the NT would automatically see the word *prophecy* as having diametrically opposed meanings when referring to Old Testament prophecy (*infallible*) versus New Testament prophecy (*fallible*). By retooling the meaning and definition of such a central word as prophecy, the doctrine of *fallible prophecy* creates a host of doctrinal problems and points of confusion within the church, raising questions about the nature of the God who promises that His revealed word will not return to Him empty without accomplishing what He desires (Isaiah 55:11).

- By restructuring the ancient definition of prophecy, the doctrine of *fallible prophecy* effectively re-labels what the Scriptures define as a false prophet.

[13] Wayne A. Grudem, <u>Systematic Theology</u>, (Grand Rapids: MI, Zondervan Publishing, 1994), 1057.

This dangerously opens the door of the church to "enthusiasts or deceivers."[14] Moreover, the Old Testament and New Testament Scriptures remind us that there are prescribed tests[15] that must be employed in order to determine if a prophet was true or false. Such tests not only revealed the character of the supposed prophet, but they especially exposed the affections of those who either applied or ignored such tests. It is my contention that the redefinitions supplied by the doctrine of *fallible prophecy* nearly eradicate such prescribed tests, thus exposing the body of Christ to innumerable temptations and dangers.

- Within the system of *fallible prophecy*, members are instructed to sift through the words of any prophecy with the understanding that an admixture of truth and error will flow from the "legitimate" NT prophet. Depending on the nature of such an admixture, some or all of a spoken prophecy could be rejected based upon such an analysis. Apart from a clear contradiction to Scripture, personal prophecies have little objective criteria by which they can be measured, leaving the hearer with a great potential for confusion and uncertainty.

- In light of the above point, it should be noted that the consciences of believers can be unnecessarily bound by supposed prophecies that cannot be fully and objectively evaluated. Thus, believers who are prophetically exhorted to make significant choices are left with the task of discerning if it is the Holy Spirit, or the "fallible prophet," who has spoken to them. In view of this, there is a great potential for doubt and uncertainty among those who desire to obey God under the guidance of *fallible prophecy*.

- Within the doctrine of *fallible prophecy*, Agabus is traditionally utilized as the central example of a NT fallible prophet (Acts 21:10-11). However, there are several inconsistencies concerning the interpretation and application of his example. If Agabus' example was followed logically (according to the logic of *fallible prophecy*), then no *fallible prophecy*

---

[14] Charles Hodge, <u>Commentary on Romans</u>, (Wheaton Ill: Crossway Books, 1993), Romans 12:6.

[15] 1 John 4:1.

would ever require obedience from a believer due to the corrupting presence of error. This reality guts *fallible prophecy* of any positive value or purpose whatsoever.

- From the standard of Scripture, it was no small thing for a person to claim to be a prophet of God. The Bible explicitly affirms only two classes of prophets: *true prophets and false prophets.* In the Old Testament, the penalty of death fell upon those who falsely claimed such a gift and office. However, according to the doctrine of *fallible prophecy*, neither grave error nor immaturity should serve as a barrier to the exercise of such a gift by *nearly everyone*[16] within the local church. Such thinking is a tragedy for the body of Christ which is called to holiness and truth in all aspects of life and servitude.

- In the New Testament we see repeated lessons on the supremacy of the New Covenant over the Old Covenant, yet how does a degraded form of prophecy (*fallible New Testament prophecy*) demonstrate such supremacy?

There are many details that have yet to be unfolded, but the above summary gives us some important thoughts and questions that will guide our thinking as we examine the subject of *fallible prophecy*. As we look at the subject of *fallible prophecy*, our main analysis will be directed towards the writings of Wayne Grudem. The reason for this is that the volume of Grudem's writings on this subject far outweighs that of any other within the realm of *continuationist* authors such as Jack Deere, D.A. Carson, and John Piper. The specific works of Grudem that will receive central attention are his *Systematic Theology* (Zondervan Publishing House, 1994) and his book, *The Gift of Prophecy in the New Testament and Today* (Crossway Books, 2000).

---

[16] More will be said about this in chapter 4, but Wayne Grudem repeatedly argues that nearly all in the church can and should seek to employ this gift. He falls short of saying that everyone can and will, but he so emphasizes the universal pursuit of prophesy, that he resultantly argues *almost all* can exercise the gift of prophecy.

I should remind the reader that there have been several, excellent critiques of Grudem published over the past several years. In fact, the quantity and quality of these works raises the question: *why write a complete book on the subject of fallible prophecy?* The answer to this is twofold. First, there are four published works to which I will refer in this book that are quite excellent and thorough:

Robert L. Thomas, *Prophecy Rediscovered? A Review of The Gift of Prophecy in the New Testament and Today* (Bibliotheca Sacra #149).

F. David Farnell, *Fallible New Testament Prophecy/Prophets? A Critique of Wayne Grudem's Hypothesis* (Master's Seminary Journal 2:2, Fall 1991).

Dr. R. Bruce Compton, *The Continuation of New Testament Prophecy and a Closed Canon: A Critique of Wayne Grudem's Two Levels of New Testament Prophecy* (Detroit Baptist Theological Seminary).

Thomas R. Edgar, *Satisfied by the Promise of the Spirit*, Kregel Resources Grand Rapids MI, 1996.[17]

Because Grudem has already responded to the majority of arguments presented in these works (among others), there remains a need for an argumentative redress. It should be self-evident to the reader that, by generating this book, I am not answering for the above writers, nor do I wish to convey the thought that their works are somehow deficient. Yet, I have written this book because Grudem's responses to these men raise a full spectrum of *new questions* about the reasoning and practice of *fallible prophecy.* Secondly, I would submit that there are broader concerns that must be addressed concerning prophecy – concerns that go beyond what Grudem's critics have written to date. It is in this sense that I hope to

---

[17] Though there are other published contributions to this debate, the four listed works offer an excellent, sufficient, and available sampling that the reader can access online quite easily.

present to the reader some new, big-picture queries regarding the world of *fallible prophecy.*

Since Grudem's work on the subject of *fallible prophecy* has been extensive, he will remain the primary focus of our analysis. In summary form, our examination of *fallible prophecy* will be simplified to the following points of analysis and critique:

1. Chapter 1: Prophecy – A Test of Love: According to the proponents of *fallible prophecy,* the presence of error in a prophetic utterance does not make such claimants of the prophetic gift false prophets, it only means that they are *New Testament fallible prophets, by definition.* It is my contention that this constitutes a complete reversal of meaning of *prophecy* which results in a confused message concerning the nature and character of the God who has consistently and effectually revealed Himself through His appointed messengers. Moreover, such a redaction of prophecy effectively confuses, and nearly eliminates, the scripturally prescribed tests for prophecy. The importance of this must not be underestimated, for all of the tests of prophecy, in the Old Testament and the New Testament, have an unimpeachable centerpiece: the love of God.

2. Chapter 2: Fallible prophecy – Lexical Considerations: Grudem argues that the New Testament connotation of the word prophet no longer possessed the sense of authority it once had. Thus, Christ did not call his disciples *prophets* because "...the Greek word *prophētēs* ('prophet') at the time of the New Testament...did not have the sense 'one who speaks God's very words'."[18] In view of Grudem's emphasis on this point, it will be very important for us to examine his lexical justification for such a conclusion.

3. Chapter 3: Fallible prophecy – The Case of Agabus: Grudem argues that *genuine* NT prophets could be resisted in view of their fallibility: "When Paul says, 'Let two or three prophets speak, and *let the others weigh what is said*' (1

---

[18] Grudem, <u>Systematic Theology</u>, 1050.

Cor. 14:29), he suggests that they should listen carefully and sift the good from the bad, accepting some and rejecting the rest (for this is the implication of the Greek word *diakrinō*, here translated 'weigh what is said')."[19] In support of this position, Grudem supplies examples of what he believes are NT fallible prophets, the most central of which is Agabus. Like Grudem, D.A. Carson insists that Agabus' prophecy was fraught with error, saying, "I can think of no reported Old Testament prophet whose prophecies are so wrong on the details."[20] This is a strong charge requiring careful evaluation.

4. Chapter 4: Fallible prophecy – A Gift for All?: Grudem argues that, unlike the unique gift of prophecy given in the time of the OT, the NT gift of prophecy was extremely common and functioned "in thousands of ordinary Christians in hundreds of local churches at the time of the New Testament."[21] As well, such New Testament prophecy did not supply divine revelation, instead "...the words 'prophet' and 'prophecy' are used more commonly to refer to ordinary Christians who spoke not with absolute divine authority but simply to report something that God had brought to their minds." For him, this argues against the gift as having a foundational role (Ephesians 2:20 and 3:5).

5. Conclusion: The Fallible Prophets of New Calvinism: Believing in the value and efficacy of *fallible prophecy,* a growing number of popular pastors and teachers are now openly promoting such teaching. Particularly within the increasingly popular *New Calvinism* movement we find a growing number of advocates of *fallible prophecy.* To facilitate the spread of this doctrine Grudem himself supplies a 6-point strategy for establishing *fallible prophecy* within the local church. This poses an increasing danger of the tolerance and proliferation of false prophets within the church.

It is my contention that this contemporary theology is neither benign nor harmless. Its complete reversal of the meaning of prophecy plants within

---

[19] Ibid., 1054.

[20] Wayne Grudem, The Gift of Prophecy in the New Testament and Today (Revised Edition) (IL: Wheaton, Crossway Books, Kindle Edition, 2000), 80.

[21] Ibid., 286.

the church a dangerous seed of thought and practice. Having said this I must also recognize that not all those who identify with the label *New Calvinism* necessarily agree with the doctrine of *fallible prophecy.* The title of this book is *The Fallible Prophets of New Calvinism* for this simple reason: *many* of the assumed leaders of the *New Calvinism* movement believe, teach, and advocate the doctrine of *fallible prophecy*, yet I have found that some who wish to call themselves *New* or *Neo Calvinists* are not aware of this connection with *fallible prophecy.* Therefore, my appeal to the reader is to consider this significant context when they attempt to identify themselves theologically by such labels.

At the beginning of this introduction, I mentioned my sense of fatigue over the writing of polemical works. I meant this in the sense of Jude's redirect from writing about "our common salvation" to that of an earnest appeal to the church because certain false teachers who "crept in unnoticed" into the church. By drawing this analogy, I am not likening the advocates of *fallible prophecy* to the apostates described by Jude, but I am expressing a desire to press on to other foci of writing and preaching. Yet, I am persuaded that the subject of *fallible prophecy* is quite grave and, though it does not rise to the level of Jude's wrap-sheet of apostates, I do maintain that it plants a dangerous seed of corruption within the church. Moreover, it is a teaching that is both seductive and attractive for many reasons, not the least of which is the strong support that it receives from popular men like C. Peter Wagner, Jack Deere, D.A. Carson, Wayne Grudem, and John Piper. Especially with respect to the last three men, their popularity and centrality to the recent movement called *New Calvinism* continues to spread the teachings of *continuationism* (and along with it, *fallible prophecy*) at an alarming rate. Overall, Grudem's *Systematic Theology* continues to grow in its popularity and influence such that 450,000 copies have been sold to date. The breadth of its influence continues to grow seeing that it has been translated into eight other languages, with at least eight more foreign translations now in process. Unfortunately, I must also report that my Alma Mater (The Master's Seminary) has used Wayne Grudem's *Systematic Theology* for several years, even though the institution represents a cessationistic point of view, one that is incompatible with *fallible prophecy*.[22] As a pastor, I see the consequences and influences of these choices quite frequently, especially when others appear incredulous when exposed to Grudem's, Carson's, and Piper's views on spiritual gifts and *fallible prophecy*. The influence of such teaching continues to spread in great measure and it must therefore be confronted with unwavering conviction. To this end, we must recognize that what is needful is a sound and well-reasoned examination of the Scriptures on the subject of *fallible prophecy*. However, it would be utterly useless, even dangerous, to focus our attention on the most extreme and outlier examples of the continuationist movement such that we lose sight of those problematic influences which quietly infiltrate the body of Christ without detection or warning. What we must remember is that the doctrine of the Spirit, along with His gifts given to the church, must be handled with great care and attention. Far above this author's best efforts, the reader should consider John Owen's classic work, *Discourse on the Holy Spirit*, where Owen heralds the beauty and centrality of the Holy Spirit's presence and work in the life of all true believers:

---

[22] By mentioning this fact, it is not my intention to suggest that The Master's Seminary (TMS) is attempting to spread Grudem's doctrine of fallible prophecy. I am arguing that there are far better resources available, especially in view of the many time-tested works used by conservative seminaries throughout the years. Though TMS is only using portions of Grudem's Systematic Theology, I am concerned that it is being used at all. His views on the Holy Spirit and the efficacy of God's revelation permeate many other topics beyond that of spiritual gifts. Grudem's writings continue to increase in their popularity and influence, often leading to tolerance or acceptance of his more problematic teachings. It is this indirect and mediated influence that concerns me the most because it is so subtle and often undetected.

"...whatever men may pretend, unto this day, 'if they have not the Spirit of Christ, they are none of his,' Rom. viii. 9: for our Lord Jesus Christ hath promised him as a comforter, to abide with his disciples forever, John xiv. 16, and by him it is that he is present with them and among them to the end of the world, Matt. xxviii. 20, xviii. 20;... [by the Holy Spirit] we are enabled to believe, and are made partakers of that holiness without which no man shall see God. Wherefore, without him all religion is but a body without a soul, a carcass without an animating spirit. It is true, in the continuation of his work he ceaseth from putting forth those extraordinary effects of his power which were needful for the laying the foundation of the church in the world; but the whole work of his grace, according to the promise of the covenant, is no less truly and really carried on at this day, in and towards all the elect of God, than it was on the day of Pentecost and onwards; and so is his communication of gifts necessary for the edification of the church, Eph. iv. 11-13. The owning, therefore, and avowing the work of the Holy Ghost in the hearts and on the minds of men, according to the tenor of the covenant of grace, is the principal part of that profession which at this day all believers are called unto."[23]

"A full and clear declaration from the Scripture of the nature of the Holy Spirit and his operations may, through the blessing of God, be of use to fortify the minds of professors against satanical delusions counterfeiting his actings and inspirations; for directions unto this purpose are given us by the holy apostle, who lived to see great havoc made in the churches by deluding spirits. Knowledge of the truth, trying of spirits that go abroad by the doctrines of the Scriptures, dependence on the Holy Spirit for his teachings according to the word, are the things which to this purpose he commends unto us."[24]

With much gravity, Owen reveals the danger that awaits those who make false claims to the prophetic gift. Moreover, he reveals the great danger that comes to God's people through such prophetic imposters. In view of this historic advancement of the false claimants of prophecy, the church

---

[23] John Owen, The Works of John Owen, ed. William H. Goold, (Edinburgh, UK: The Banner of Truth Trust, 1988), 3:154-155.
[24] Ibid., 36.

must be on guard, seeing that Satan's agenda to obfuscate divine revelation continues with increasing ferocity. As the church presses on in this contest over truth, she must never doubt the sufficiency, power, and authority of God's word for her cleansing, sanctification, and protection.

As already mentioned, this book cannot cover every modern aberration of the doctrine of prophecy, but will focus on the chief concerns that come with the contemporary teachings of *fallible prophecy*. Lest the reader be confused at the outset, I am writing as one who believes fully in the continued power and working of the Holy Spirit in Christ's church; I write as one who believes in the absolute sovereignty of God who will do all His good pleasure in His good time; and I believe that the canon of Scripture supplies the church with all that it needs, and though the apostles and prophets of the early church are not with us today, their authoritative ministry continues because of the living and active word of God. I am appealing that we all seek to comprehend more fully the riches that we possess in the person of the Holy Spirit and the completed canon of Scripture as delivered by the apostles and prophets, Christ Jesus being the very cornerstone. Above and beyond the polemic nature of our study, let us rejoice in the perfection of all that God has sufficiently supplied for His people.

Finally, and as previously mentioned, the reader should know that it is not my position that *fallible prophecy* constitutes an immediate assault on the Gospel. Yet, it is my contention that *fallible prophecy* supplies a dangerous detour for the modern church, one that has a great potential for undermining our core understanding of the nature of God Himself. Where this detour will ultimately lead in the future is a question that remains unanswered, yet I hope to show the reader that *fallible prophecy* supplies a serious denigration of God's character through a serious redaction of His sovereign gift of prophecy. Such an error as this has the potential of leading others into a state of confusion, leading to doubt concerning the certitude and blessing of all that God has effectually revealed. Additionally, by offering this critique it is not my intention to disparage all of the teachings and convictions of those who hold to *fallible prophecy*. It may be that those reading this book have profited from the teachings of various men named within the pages of this critique. My point is not to disregard that which is profitable, but to express concern for that which is unprofitable leaving the final judgment of all things to God alone. Additionally, the church should be on guard concerning the integral problem of *Evangelical celebritism*[25] which plagues the body of Christ with several, unwholesome influences in the modern day. In many cases, such *celebritism* serves as the vehicle for problematic teachings like *fallible prophecy*, whether such an influence is intended or unintended. In the end, this book is designed to herald God's truth, not Evangelical celebrities.

My great concern is that the modern church will have to face the rising influences of *fallible prophecy*, and if she is not prepared for the onslaught of this influence, many will be led astray in ways that are difficult to estimate.

May Christ alone be exalted in His church.

---

[25] I acknowledge that the word *celebritism* is an invention, however, it is a recognized *urban term* that speaks of the slavish devotion of the masses to those who are deemed celebrities, whether secular or religious. It represents a very real problem and for this reason, I employ it as a legitimate term.

CHAPTER 1:

PROPHECY – A TEST

OF LOVE

As we begin our study of prophecy, great care must be taken so that we would not miss the "big picture" of such a subject. What a shame it would be if we scrutinized the minutia of this debate, while failing to see the "forest for the trees" as the expression goes. It is out of this very concern that I wish to present the reader with some broader, scriptural themes that will aid us in our consideration of the subject of prophecy. In fact, the principles that we will be reviewing in this chapter will weave an important thread throughout the entire book. In this chapter, we will examine God's valuation of His gift of prophecy, without which we would be lost in our estimation of the subject at hand. Thus, we will first consider how it is that God's gift of prophecy reveals His sovereign, omnipotent, and infallible character. Secondly, we will consider how God's prophetic word supplies an important test for the community of God's own people. Both of these considerations will prove to be essential for everything else that follows in this book.

Prophecy and the Nature of God

God so closely identifies Himself with His revealed word that the incarnate Son of God is Himself identified, by name, as *the Word*.[26] Such a name as this reminds us that the purity, veracity, and perfection of God's revelation must never be compared to the trifle words of mere men and their impotent idols.[27] It is therefore crucial to recognize that God's revelatory gift of prophecy tells us essential things about the nature of God Himself. Unlike the host of *false and fallible prophets* who represent their *false and fallible deities*, God's true prophets have been sent throughout history in order to convey God's magisterial authority and sovereignty over all of His creation, as the Lord sovereignly declared through His prophet Isaiah:

---

[26] John 1:1-14, Revelation 19:13.

[27] Jeremiah 10.

Isaiah 55:10–11: 10 "For as the rain and the snow come down from heaven, And do not return there without watering the earth And making it bear and sprout, and furnishing seed to the sower and bread to the eater; 11 "So will My word be which goes forth from My mouth; It will not return to Me empty, without accomplishing what I desire, and without succeeding in the matter for which I sent it."

These powerful verses establish a crucial lesson: God never misspeaks, nor does He stutter with ineffectual musings, instead His spoken word *directly* and *effectually* reveals His power and authority seeing that even the heavens were made *by the word of the Lord.*[28] God's miraculous use of *fallible men* to communicate His *infallible word* spans revelatory history, leading to the most central moment in all of God's providence:

Hebrews 1:1–4: 1 God, after He spoke long ago to the fathers in the prophets in many portions and in many ways, 2 in these last days has spoken to us in His Son, whom He appointed heir of all things, through whom also He made the world. 3 And He is the radiance of His glory and the exact representation of His nature, and upholds all things by the word of His power. When He had made purification of sins, He sat down at the right hand of the Majesty on high, 4 having become as much better than the angels, as He has inherited a more excellent name than they.

These introductory texts help us to see God's purpose and valuation of the gift of prophecy throughout the ages. All of God's divine revelation serves the *unhindered* purpose of heralding God's glory and majesty, which is consummately revealed in His Son. Hebrews 1:1-4 reminds us that every facet of God's revelation discloses, without hindrance, the Messiah, whose authority and power is infinitely greater than that of the angels in Heaven. Overall, God has revealed these truths *in many portions and in many ways*, but through it all we see the glorious omnipotence of the One whose word does not return to Him void. Similarly, John points

---

[28] Psalm 33:6, John 1:3.

to Christ's centrality in all of God's revelation with remarkable brevity and power:

> John 1:17–18: 17 For the Law was given through Moses; grace and truth were realized through Jesus Christ. 18 No one has seen God at any time; the only begotten God who is in the bosom of the Father, He has explained Him.

Like our text in Hebrews, John reminds us that Jesus Christ is the centerpiece of all of God's revelation. When John wrote these words, he faced a religious culture that sinfully exalted God's messengers (like Moses) over the Lord and His word. This failure to honor the purpose and message of Scripture revealed serious corruption, warranting a grave rebuke from the Savior:

> John 5:45–47: 45 "Do not think that I will accuse you before the Father; the one who accuses you is Moses, in whom you have set your hope. 46 "For if you believed Moses, you would believe Me, for he wrote about Me. 47 "But if you do not believe his writings, how will you believe My words?"

Please notice that Christ does not say that the Jews placed their hope in the *writings* of Moses, instead, He accused them of placing their hope in Moses himself. Thus, they were not God-centered in their religious devotion; rather, they were deeply man-centered. Within such a rebuke Christ equated Moses' *writings* with His own words, thus reminding them that Moses delivered God's direct revelation about the Lord Jesus Christ. To the 1st century Jewish community the teachings of Christ were earth shattering. The Savior's teaching revealed to them that God's revelation has always served the *effectual and unhindered* purpose of magnifying the Lord such that every law; every historical narrative; every divine ordinance; every ceremony, sacrifice and moral code, sovereignly delivered by God's messengers, had but one agenda – to direct men to the supremacy and majesty of the Lord Jesus Christ. In all of this I believe that we can confess that God is a God who does not misspeak when granting the revelatory gift of prophecy. Clearly, Old Testament history reveals that the variance of God's servants and messengers is striking, but what He accomplishes through them is the same: *unhindered divine revelation.* He has spoken through multiple prophets and unique leaders (like Abraham and Moses) in order to disclose His revelation; He has used the wicked to declare His word and can use asses and rocks to render utterances that are pleasing to Him. Overall, despite creaturely frailty and fallibility, God has used kings, priests, judges, and prophets to disclose the glory of the One who is the King of kings and Lord of lords; the Prophet; our Great High Priest; the uniquely chosen Servant; and returning Judge – Jesus Christ. When we pause and consider the collective force of all these principles, we learn an essential lesson about the character and nature of God: He is utterly sovereign in the delivery of His infallible message – a message that supplies the bedrock of real assurance to believers of all generations, in the Old Covenant and the New:

> 2 Peter 1:16–21: 16 For we did not follow cleverly devised tales when we made known to you the power and coming of our Lord Jesus Christ, but we were eyewitnesses of His majesty. 17 For when He received honor and glory from God the Father, such an utterance as this was made to Him by the Majestic Glory, "This is My beloved Son with whom I am well-pleased"— 18 and we ourselves heard this utterance made from heaven when we were with Him on the holy mountain. 19 So we have the prophetic word made more sure, to which you do well to pay attention as to a lamp shining in a dark place, until the day dawns and the morning star arises in your hearts. 20 But know this first of all, that no prophecy of Scripture is a matter of one's own interpretation, 21 for no prophecy was ever made by an act of human will, but men moved by the Holy Spirit spoke from God.

Clearly, Peter wanted his audience to know that what was being revealed to the New Testament church was not a fabrication of human invention. To do this, Peter reminded his readers of God's nature and sovereign work through His chosen messengers. God's actions throughout history have been delivered through the *perfectly trustworthy record of Scripture* because *no prophecy was ever made by an act of human will, but men moved by the Holy Spirit spoke from God.* Simply put, this is how God works. Our Lord is the same yesterday, today, and forever and He takes His revelation very seriously. Throughout history, God's prophetic revelation has been central to this precious matter of revealing the glory of Christ. Additionally, God's gift of prophetic revelation has been central to the salvation, sanctification, and confirmation of His people within this fallen world. Those who cherish and obey His word reveal themselves to be His children,[29] but those who pursue other voices reveal a different spiritual pedigree.[30] In this sense, God's word is like a magnet: it draws and attracts God's children, while repelling those who are not His. It is in this sense that God's word supplies a crucial, polarizing test among those who claim to be the followers of God.

Prophecy – A Test of Love

God's word sharply polarizes and divides the true church from the false. It is a two edged sword that divides and exposes truth from error. It is for this reason that Paul enjoined Timothy to preach, not the mythologies of men, but the word alone, knowing that there will always be those whose appetites are never satisfied unless they accumulate for themselves teachers in accordance to their own desires.[31] This is why Peter explained to his readers the nature of genuine prophecy 2 Peter 1:16-21. This served as an important foundation for his warning regarding Satan's coordinated agenda to impersonate and corrupt God's prophetic revelation:

> 2 Peter 2:1: 1 But false prophets also arose among the people, just as there will also be false teachers among you, who will secretly introduce destructive

---

[29] John 14:21, 1 John 2:3.

[30] 1 John 2:18-20.

[31] 2 Timothy 4:2-4.

heresies, even denying the Master who bought them, bringing swift destruction upon themselves.

One thing that we know about Satan is that he cleverly operates by stealth. This is how his messengers arise among the people, secretly introducing destructive heresies. They do not enter the assembly of God's people announcing their spiritual and spoken corruptions; instead, they enter in sheep's clothing.[32] This poses no surprise to the student of Scripture since the serpent (Satan) was called "more crafty than any beast of the field" (Genesis 3). His heresies were introduced in the garden, not overtly, but covertly, incrementally, and deceptively with an admixture of truth and error. Biblical history reveals that God has sovereignly delivered His perfect word to His people, yet this same history reveals that Satan has been there every step of the way, looking to corrupt and pollute that which God has delivered through His appointed messengers. Which brings us to the subject of prophecy as *a test of love*. Without this central consideration, we would miss the forest for the trees. God calls His people to discern between His divine revelation versus those who foment cleverly devised tales and destructive heresies; yet such a pursuit of discernment must be handled with great care. God's people are known as those who rely on the authority of God *alone*.[33] This they do as an expression of love for Him. However, God's people must do this with caution, understanding that the pursuit of discernment *alone* can lead to a heartless exercise:

> Revelation 2:1–4: 1 "To the angel of the church in Ephesus write: The One who holds the seven stars in His right hand, the One who walks among the seven golden lampstands, says this: 2 'I know your deeds and your toil and perseverance, and that you cannot tolerate evil men, and you put to the test those who call themselves apostles, and they are not, and you found them to be false; 3 and you have perseverance and have endured for My name's sake, and

---

[32] Matthew 7:15.
[33] Psalm 119:92.

have not grown weary. 4 'But I have this against you, that you have left your first love.

Christ's solemn warning is deeply instructive, revealing the centrality of love in everything. The church at Ephesus believed that they were doing well. Their discernment skills revealed much in the way of their knowledge; however, sadly, they had lost sight of the centerpiece of everything. Discernment over God's revelation is absolutely crucial, but we must not lose the centerpiece of love for God in any way. It is this same emphasis on the centrality of love that we find throughout the Old and New Testament. Remember that it was the Savior who cited Deuteronomy 6:4-5 and Leviticus 19:18 when He gave these instructions concerning the foremost commandment:

Mark 12:28–31: 28 One of the scribes came and heard them arguing, and recognizing that He had answered them well, asked Him, "What commandment is the foremost of all?" 29 Jesus answered, "The foremost is, 'HEAR, O ISRAEL! THE LORD OUR GOD IS ONE LORD; 30 AND YOU SHALL LOVE THE LORD YOUR GOD WITH ALL YOUR HEART, AND WITH ALL YOUR SOUL, AND WITH ALL YOUR MIND, AND WITH ALL YOUR STRENGTH.' 31 "The second is this, 'YOU SHALL LOVE YOUR NEIGHBOR AS YOURSELF.' There is no other commandment greater than these."

If there is a central motive and affection emphasized within the full corpus of Holy Writ, it is love. The harmony of this theme is transcendently beautiful, reminding us that whatever we do in life, if it is not done out of love for the Lord first then our servitude is counted as nothing. This precious standard of love also supplies a warning to those who are inclined to tolerate and endure those messengers whom God has not sent to His people:

Deuteronomy 13:1–5: 1 "If a prophet or a dreamer of dreams arises among you and gives you a sign or a wonder, 2 and the sign or the wonder comes true, concerning which he spoke to you, saying, 'Let us go after other gods (whom you have not known) and let us serve them,' 3 you shall not listen to the words of that prophet or that dreamer of dreams; for the LORD your God is testing you to find out if you love the LORD your God with all your heart and with all your soul. 4 "You shall follow the LORD your God and fear Him; and you shall keep His commandments, listen to His voice, serve Him, and cling to Him. 5 "But that prophet or that dreamer of dreams shall be put to death, because he has counseled rebellion against the LORD your God who brought you from the land of Egypt and redeemed you from the house of slavery, to seduce you from the way in which the LORD your God commanded you to walk. So you shall purge the evil from among you.

I would ask the reader to consider the central test supplied in Deuteronomy 13:3. We would miss too much if we only gleaned from this passage the specific tests supplied for evaluating a claimant of the prophetic gift. Though extremely important, those tests are only a subordinate component of God's broader test for His people, as He said: *for the LORD your God is testing you to find out if you love the LORD your God with all your heart and with all your soul.* As a messenger of Satan, the false prophet was introduced within the community of God's people in order to seduce them from the way in which the LORD God commanded them to walk. Therefore, acceptance or even toleration of such an errorist revealed a lack of love for the one true God. As already discussed, God cherishes His word and desires genuine devotion from His people through His divine revelation:

Hosea 4:6 "My people are destroyed for lack of knowledge…"

Hosea 6:6: "For I delight in loyalty rather than sacrifice, And in the knowledge of God rather than burnt offerings."

Without the Lord's revealed word, there can be no knowledge of Him or genuine loyalty. Without such knowledge of Him, we are destroyed amidst the innumerable idols crafted by our own vain imagination. Throughout history, God has used the revelation of His word as a central means by which He would be known and His worshippers would be made evident amidst this idol-filled world. Those who genuinely herald God and His word are revealed to be those who love Him truly; those who tolerate error and the corruptions of God's revelation simply fail such a test of love. This is why the prescribed tests for prophets were so important for the people of God. The severe consequences which fell to those who were found to be false prophets should remind us of the importance of such tests:

Deuteronomy 18:18–22: 18 "I will raise up a prophet from among their countrymen like you, and I will put My words in his mouth, and he shall speak to them all that I command him. 19 "It shall come about that whoever will not listen to My words which he shall speak in My name, I Myself will require it of him. 20 "But the prophet who speaks a word presumptuously in My name which I have not commanded him to speak, or which he speaks in the name of other gods, that prophet shall die." 21 "You may say in your heart, 'How will we know the word which the LORD has not spoken?' 22 "When a prophet speaks in the name of the LORD, if the thing does not come about or come true, that is the thing which the LORD has not spoken. The prophet has spoken it presumptuously; you shall not be afraid of him."

Jeremiah 14:13–15: 13 But, "Ah, Lord GOD!" I said, "Look, the prophets are telling them, 'You will not see the sword nor will you have famine, but I will give you lasting peace in this place.' " 14 Then the LORD said to me, "The prophets are prophesying falsehood in My name. I have neither sent them nor commanded them nor spoken to them; they are prophesying to you a false vision, divination, futility and the deception of their own minds. 15 "Therefore thus says the LORD concerning the prophets who are prophesying in My name, although it was not I who sent them—yet they keep saying, 'There will be no sword or famine in this land'—by sword and famine those prophets shall meet their end!

When we compare Deuteronomy 13:1-5, 18:18-22, and Jeremiah 14:13-16, the following standards emerge:

1. A prophet was to be executed if he directed the people to other gods, even if he performed a sign or wonder that came true (Deut 13:1-2).

2. A prophet was to be executed if he spoke presumptuously in God's name (Deut. 18:20a, Jeremiah 14:13–16).

3. A prophet was to be executed if he spoke in the name of other gods (Deut. 18:20b).

4. A prophet whose prophecy was found to be false was to be executed as one who spoke presumptuously (Deut.18:21-22, Jeremiah 14:13–16).

Upon closer examination of the supplied tests, points 1 and 3, along with 2 and 4, share common ideas. In points 1 and 3, the common denominator is that of idolatry, though point 1 reminds us that the working of signs and wonders offers no help for such a heretic:

Matthew 24:24: For false Christs and false prophets will arise and will show great signs and wonders, so as to mislead, if possible, even the elect.

Christ's warning to His disciples is well rooted in the ancient truth of Deuteronomy 13:1-5. Thus, out of love for the Savior, the believer must remember that no sign or wonder can cover the corruptions and idolatries of a false prophet. Both tests (1 and 3) also remind us that prophets were to be evaluated in light of the possibility of idolatry. The means by which such an analysis was to be done was through God's already revealed word. Clearly, the introduction of other deities stood in violation of God's principal commandment within the Decalogue: *you shall have no other gods before me.* Failure to adhere to these standards revealed a failure of God's ultimate test of love. As we move on in the list, we see that points 2 and 4 focus on the idea of presumption. The evidence of a false prophecy revealed to all that the self-professed prophet was acting with such presumption. This word *presumption* (H. *ziyḏ*) is an important term in the Law and wisdom literature. In its root meaning it refers to the act of boiling.[34] When used of men, it refers to a seething/boiling pride, arrogance, insolence, or even rage, whereby "The basic idea is pride, a sense of self-importance, which often is exaggerated to include defiance and even rebelliousness."[35] Such a term as this refers to a man who is not interested in the genuine authority of God Himself:

Deuteronomy 17:12: "The man who *acts presumptuously* [*ḇezāḏŏn*] by not listening to the priest who stands there to serve the LORD your God, nor to the judge, that man shall die; thus you shall purge the evil from Israel." (italics mine).

Proverbs 21:24: "'Proud,' 'Haughty,' 'Scoffer,' are his names, Who acts with *insolent pride [zāḏŏn]*." (italics mine).

As it relates to the tests for prophecy, we should note that such tests not only scrutinized the words of the self-professed prophet, but they also scrutinized the individual's character. The presence of pride and self-importance revealed that the so-called prophet was no servant of God. Prophets of this order may *intend* to mislead others or perhaps they are *self-deceived*. In either case, they are called presumptuous because, despite their claims, God did not speak to them at all. If the error of their words were not known immediately by the people, then the corruption of their lives would become evident in time, as the Savior Himself said:

---

[34] Esau craved Jacob's "boiled" [*nāziyḏ*] stew: Genesis 25:29.

[35] R. Laird Harris, Gleason L. Archer, Jr., Bruce K. Waltke, eds., <u>The Theological Wordbook of the Old Testament</u> (Chicago: Moody Press, 1980), 2:238.

Matthew 7:15–16:   15 "Beware of the false prophets, who come to you in sheep's clothing, but inwardly are ravenous wolves. 16 "You will know them by their fruits. Grapes are not gathered from thorn bushes nor figs from thistles, are they?"

In the Old Testament and in the New, all of the prophetic tests have the design to reveal much more than just the words of a self-proclaimed prophet; their actions must be scrutinized as well. Moreover, it wasn't just the prophet who was thus scrutinized, but God tests His people in view of their *action* or *inaction* concerning such imposters. The action required of Old Testament saints was most grave. When the claimant of prophecy was found to be false, "that prophet shall die" (Deut. 18:20) and "So you shall purge the evil from among you" (Deut. 13:5). This important and familiar expression is found within the book of Deuteronomy ten times. In all but one text, it refers to removal of the wicked by execution. Though this expression is used in the New Testament, its application was different from that of the Old Covenant. In the New Covenant of Christ's blood, Gospel mercy through church discipline became the new standard for this ancient expression:

1 Corinthians 5:12–13:   12 For what have I to do with judging outsiders? Do you not judge those who are within the church? 13 But those who are outside, God judges. REMOVE THE WICKED [*ponēron*] MAN FROM AMONG YOURSELVES.

By the standard of the New Covenant, the expression, "remove the wicked [G. *ponēron*] from among you" no longer denotes execution; instead it refers to excommunication from the church. Thus, the NT church was forbidden to fellowship with or tolerate those who were found to be false professors (wicked/evil [*ponēron*]). This included false prophets whom the church was ordered to expose by means of testing:

1 John 4:1: Beloved, do not believe every spirit, but test the spirits to see whether they are from God, because many false prophets have gone out into the world.

Within the early church, the tares of proto-Gnostic teachers and prophets plagued the landscape. Many of these individuals, who crept into the church unnoticed would not be easily detected since they spoke, in abundance, of Christ, sin, grace, salvation, and the true knowledge of God. However, their denial of core doctrines of Scripture meant that their utterances consisted of a corrupted mixture of truth and error. John's call for discernment should remind us that the challenges confronting the early church are no different today. In all generations, the evaluation and testing of prophets was to be done out of a love for the Lord and for His truth - *without compromise*. Loveless discernment leads to the error of those who were rebuked at Ephesus. However, failure to apply God's prescribed tests at all constitutes a grave failure of love for God and His word (Matthew 24:24, 1 John 4:1, Deut. 13:1-5, 18:18-22, John 14:21). It is absolutely crucial that we understand the central test of love in Deuteronomy 13:1-5: God's agenda was to expose the heart of the people through their *action* or *inaction* in response to the claimant of prophecy. Our aforementioned text of Jeremiah 14:13-15 leads us to a similar and stark conclusion:

Jeremiah 14:15–16:   15 "Therefore thus says the LORD concerning the prophets who are prophesying in My name, although it was not I who sent them—yet they keep saying, 'There will be no sword or famine in this land'—by sword and famine those prophets shall meet their end! 16 "The people also to whom they are prophesying will be thrown out into the streets of Jerusalem because of the famine and the sword; and there will be no one to bury them— neither them, nor their wives, nor their sons, nor their daughters—for I will pour out their own wickedness on them."

God's promise to "pour out their own wickedness" upon those who lend their ears to false prophets is quite grave. It shows us the severe displeasure of God over those who accept or tolerate false prophets – those to whom God has not spoken. If the people accepted or even tolerated such a false prophet, then they would be guilty of a wicked co-belligerence with such messengers. God desires that His people would know truth from error and good fruit from bad. Overall, the Lord takes His revelation very seriously. God has spoken long ago to the fathers in the prophets in many portions and in many ways, and in these last days has spoken to us in His Son. Moreover, it was not the prophets who spoke, *per se*, but the Lord Himself has spoken through His prophets. In this we see the sovereign nature of God who effectually reveals His glory through His chosen messengers. This is how God works; it is how He has revealed His sovereign majesty. The claimant of prophecy must understand the gravity that comes with the title *prophet*. It stands in history as a unique office that was designed to disclose the infallible nature of the true, self-revealing God. It is for this reason that the doctrine of *fallible prophecy* effectually obfuscates the true nature and character of the God of truth, as Robert Thomas correctly comments on the premise of *fallible prophecy*:

> "Prophecy originates in a revelation from the God of truth who cannot lie, but in the process of human transmission the prophecy may degenerate to a mistaken or erroneous report of that revelation. Yet it is difficult to see how God, who is without error, can be involved in a revelatory process that is spoiled through human imperfection."[36]

In the end, *fallible prophecy* relabels false prophecy under the pretense of a genuine gift. By redefining prophecy as that which includes both truth and error, one must wonder how any of this communicates the supremacy of Christ and the New Covenant in His blood. In all of this, a

---

[36] Thomas, <u>Prophecy Rediscovered?</u>, 87.

very crucial message begins to emerge: those who declare themselves to be a prophet of God are making an extremely serious claim. Not only was it important that such a claimant be evaluated via God's prescribed tests, but the congregation was to be tested by means of their action or inaction. In the case of their inaction, they were counted as accomplices of false prophets, worthy of the anathema of God. In everything, the Lord desires that we, in spirit and in truth, love Him above all just as the Apostle Paul instructed the Corinthian church: "If I have the gift of prophecy, and know all mysteries and all knowledge; and if I have all faith, so as to remove mountains, but do not have love, I am nothing...love does not brag, and is not arrogant, does not act unbecomingly; it does not seek its own...does not rejoice in unrighteousness, but rejoices with the truth." Without such a love for God, all that remains is God's wrath and judgment:

> 1 Corinthians 16:22: "If anyone does not love the Lord, he is to be accursed. Maranatha."

Like the foremost commandment, God's tests of prophecy have always been centered on the love of God. This chord of truth is woven throughout the Old and the New Testament, and its centrality must not be missed. It is absolutely essential that we discern God's gift of prophecy rightly and that by it we would behold the beauty and perfection of His nature which He has sovereignly revealed *without hindrance or corruption*. In all of this, we must remember that God's revelation to us *is not about us*, it is about Him and His effectual grace; it is about His matchless worth and unmitigated power; it is about His eternal glory. Unlike the imagined idols of this world, the true God of glory never misspeaks through His messengers of *divine revelation*. God has spoken clearly, and His word will not return to Him void. Should the church underestimate these crucial principles, she will be exposed to untold dangers.

Our consideration of the subject of prophecy and love supplies an essential foundation for what lies ahead. Without such a consideration of *prophecy and love*, we would be in danger of missing the broader picture of God's design for the gift of prophecy. It is this broader view of the forest that we needed to consider before inspecting the individual trees, branches, and leaves of such an important subject. All of it is God's beautiful forest of divine revelation, and He calls us to guard it with great fervency, zeal, and above all, love.

CHAPTER 2:

– FALLIBLE PROPHECY –

LEXICAL CONCERNS

In the previous chapter we considered the related discussions of *prophecy* and *love* which will serve as a necessary anchor for the remainder of our study. Within that chapter, we also considered the seriousness and gravity that comes when someone claims to be a prophet of God. Those who make such a claim are asserting that God Himself is sovereignly speaking and that they are mere human instruments in His hands. The Apostle Peter put it this way: *no prophecy was given by an act of human will, but men moved by the Holy Spirit spoke from God.*[37] It is this direct and indicative work of the Holy Spirit that characterizes genuine prophecy. However, of the false prophet God has said: *I have neither sent them nor commanded them nor spoken to them; they are prophesying to you a false vision, divination, futility and deception of their own minds.*[38] In a very simplified form, this gives us some core constructs regarding the meaning of the word *prophet.* However, a more thorough study of this term will be necessary in light of the unique definitions supplied by the proponents of *fallible prophecy.* In his *Systematic Theology* along with his book, *The Gift of Prophecy in the New Testament and Today,* Wayne Grudem argues that the New Testament reveals a complete disparity between Old Testament and New Testament prophets. The disparity in question has to do with *revelatory authority:* the New Testament prophet yields *fallible prophecies,* while the Old Testament prophet yielded prophecies that were *infallible.* Thomas Edgar summarizes matters in his book, *Satisfied by the Promise of the Spirit:*

> "Grudem has a two-pronged approach to the issue of the New Testament prophets. First, he tries to show that the apostles are equal to the Old Testament prophets. Since the New Testament prophets obviously have less authority than the apostles, the New Testament prophets likewise have less authority than the Old Testament prophets. Thus, we end up with infallible Old Testament prophets and fallible New Testament prophets. Second,

---

[37] 2 Peter 1:21.
[38] Jeremiah 14:14.

Grudem argues that the New Testament prophet is unreliable and non-authoritative..."[39]

This is no small distinction, seeing that such a disparity represents a *full reversal of meaning (fallible vs. infallible)*. It is for this reason that we must carefully consider the very lexical methodologies employed by Grudem in defense of *fallible prophecy*. To do this, we will first examine his treatment of the Greek word *prophētēs* and, secondly, we will consider his lexical and syntactic analysis of Agabus' expression: *"This is what the Holy Spirit says."*

Grudem's Lexical Treatment of prophētēs

Grudem begins his analysis by considering Christ's own method of identifying His disciples:

> "Why did Jesus choose the new term *apostle* to designate those who had the authority to write Scripture? It was probably because the Greek word *prophētēs* ('prophet') at the time of the New Testament had a very broad range of meanings. It generally did not have the sense 'one who speaks God's very words' but rather 'one who speaks on the basis of some external influence' (often spiritual influence of some kind)."[40]

In support of the above argument, Grudem cites Titus 1:12 and Luke 22:64 in order to demonstrate the breadth of meaning assigned to the word *prophet* in the "time of the New Testament" as he says.[41]

---

[39] Edgar, Satisfied by the Promise of the Spirit, (MI: Grand Rapids, Kregel Resources, 1996), 73.

[40] Grudem, Systematic Theology, 1050.

[41] Note that Grudem seeks to explain the meaning of the word *prophētēs*, not *from the New Testament*, but *in the time of the New Testament*. The distinction between these two thoughts is not small. The resources that Grudem utilizes when defining *prophētēs*, come not from the New Testament, but from extrabiblical sources *in the time of the New Testament*. It is this very distinction which yields such a different and catastrophic result.

Unfortunately for Grudem, these texts prove precious little about the word *prophētēs* except that the world was filled with an abundance of pagan notions concerning the nature of *deity, prophets,* and *prophecy*. Looking at these in order we note that, in Titus 1:12, Paul cites the Greek prophet Epimenides, who complained about his fellow Cretans, saying, "One of themselves, a prophet of their own, said, 'Cretans are always liars, evil beasts, lazy gluttons.'" All that this text demonstrates is that the Graeco-Roman world had its own collection of *false prophets, priests, and oracles* within the vast spectrum of their philosophies, mythologies, and religious beliefs. Therefore, Paul rightly refers to Epimenides as "a prophet of their own," in order to identify him has a *pagan prophet* who knew a good deal about his own Cretan culture.[42] The second text which Grudem cites, Luke 22:64, deals with the Romans who mocked Christ: "...they blindfolded Him and were asking Him, saying, 'Prophesy, who is the one who hit You?'" Grudem responds to this example by saying, "They do not mean, 'Speak words of absolute divine authority.'" We would agree, however, this example is not significantly different than Titus 1:12. The fact that the pagan world had its own notions of prophecy does not change the historic understanding of biblical prophecy. Yet Grudem further presses his argument for a secularized understanding of prophecy. To understand his argument more clearly, we will continue with his line of reasoning, as supplied in his *Systematic Theology*:

"Many writings outside the Bible use the word *prophet* (Gk. *prophētēs*) in this way, without signifying any divine authority in the words of one called a 'prophet.' In fact, by the time of the New Testament the term *prophet* in everyday use often simply meant 'one who has supernatural knowledge' or 'one who predicts the future' – or even just 'spokesman' (without any connotations of divine authority). Several examples near the time of the New Testament are given in Helmut Krämer's article in *Theological Dictionary of the New*

---

[42] 2 Timothy 4:4.

Testament are given: (footnote 2: The following examples are taken from *TDNT* 6, p. 794)

A philosopher is called 'a *prophet* of immortal nature' (Dio Chrysostom, A.D. 40-120)

A teacher (Diogenes) wants to be 'a *prophet* of truth and candor' (Lucian of Samosata, A.D. 120-180)

Those who advocate Epicurean philosophy are called '*prophets* of Epicurus' (Plutarch, A.D. 50-120)

Written history is called 'the *prophētēss* of truth' (Diodorus Siculus, wrote c. 60-30 B.C.)

A 'specialist' in botany is called a '*prophet*' (Dioscurides of Cilicia, first century A.D.)

A 'quack' in medicine is called a '*prophet*' (Galen of Pergamum, A.D. 129-199)

Krämer concludes that the Greek word for 'prophet' (*prophētēs*) 'simply expresses the formal function of declaring, proclaiming, making known.' Yet, because 'every prophet declares something which is not his own,' the Greek word for 'herald' (*keryx*) 'is the closest synonym."(footnote 3: Ibid., p. 795)."[43]

My citation of Grudem is lengthy because it is necessary for the reader to understand the full force of his analysis and methodology. Grudem consults, not the Bible, but *extrabiblical sources* in order to seek out a meaning for the word *prophētēs*, or as he puts it: "Many writings *outside the Bible* use the word prophet (Gk. *prophētēs*) in this way, without

---

[43] Grudem, Systematic Theology, 1050-51.

signifying any divine authority in the words of one called a 'prophet'" (italics mine). By going *outside the Bible*, it wouldn't be difficult at all to harvest aberrant meanings for any well-defined word. For example, one could easily achieve the same results with the Greek word, *theos (God)*.[44] When the NT writers utilized this term, they had the full force and context of OT and NT revelation which qualified the use and meaning of such a word. Thus, the meaning of this word, *theos,* when used of the true God, was *reserved and well defined* – remaining untainted by the surrounding pagan culture. However, if we were to redefine *theos* based upon *extrabiblical sources* from the Graeco-Roman world, then all kinds of thoughts and ideas would come into play – thoughts and ideas spanning the full universe of a polytheistic world, replete with *fallible deities* and their *fallible prophets.* The danger of going to extrabiblical sources, in order to discern already well-defined scriptural terms,[45] should

---

[44] In *The Gift of Prophecy in the New Testament and Today,* Grudem attempts to illustrate a similar point, yet his argument circles around his own pre-conceived assumptions about the word prophet: "Some very important words (for example, the Greek words for 'God,' 'heaven,' 'salvation,' 'church,' etc.) received greatly altered meanings from their use by the early Christians. And this could have been the same with the word 'prophet' Jesus and the New Testament authors could have retained the word if they wished and used it instead of the word 'apostle'...That could have happened, we must admit. But it didn't." Wayne Grudem. The Gift of Prophecy, 36. What Grudem fails to explain in this and other works is how this same term (*prophētēs*) was to be understood as referring to an infallible messenger when speaking of an Old Testament prophet, but infallible when speaking of a New Testament prophet. Grudem manages to avoid explaining this confusing duality of thought.

[45] Lexical analysis of any biblical word should always be thorough, incorporating a broad study of historical and contemporary-biblical uses of any word. Yet, *Scripture* itself must be given the highest priority as the standard of measurement for Scriptural words and phrases. After all, *no prophecy of Scripture is a matter of one's own interpretation* as Peter teaches us (2 Peter 1:20). Additionally, whenever the student of Scripture encounters a *hapax legomena* (a singularly occurring word in the Bible), it can become necessary to seek out extra-biblical uses of the term in order to clarify word meaning, but such a procedure must be subordinated to the word's use in the context of the biblical text itself. Thus, outside sources can be helpful in lexical analysis, but they can never substitute the

be self-evident. Sadly, this dangerous procedure is becoming more and more popular in the present day. Lexical and exegetical fallacies can come in many shapes and sizes. N.T. Wright redefines the biblical doctrine of justification by faith by redefining the word *righteousness* through the influence of the *extrabiblical, intertestamental writings of Shammaite Pharisees.* Wright's modification of just this one term enables him to overturn a deeply important doctrine which is central to the Gospel itself: *the doctrine of justification by faith alone.* Remarkably, Joseph Dillow redacts the word *metochos* (fellow partaker), *via* profane Greek uses, in

order to argue that those who don't "inherit the kingdom of heaven" can still be a Christian.[46] This tactic continues to flourish in the present day, and it is deeply dangerous.

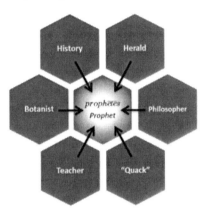

Concerning Grudem, what is especially striking about his citation of Krämer is that his list of examples of *prophētēs* is derived from page 794 of Kittel's Theological Dictionary of the New Testament (TDNT). Though I can credit him for supplying the reference, it would have been better for him to mention the section/subsection from which he harvested his data. I say this because lexical articles found within TDNT normally peruse a variety of scriptural word uses from *OT, LXX, rabbinic, intertestamental, profane Greek, and NT* sources. The value of this is that the student of Scripture can learn about the full lexical spectrum of words that are used in the Bible, from the good, bad, and ugliest examples. What is so striking about Grudem's citation is that TDNT's complete section dealing with the word

---

Scriptures as the ultimate source of context, connotation, and denotation for any biblical term.

[46] Joseph C. Dillow, The Reign of the Servant Kings (Schoettle Publishing Co. Hayseville, NC, 1992), 102-106.

prophētēs begins on page 781 and ends on page 861 of volume VI in the series – *a fairly large section for just one biblical word.*[47] Thus, for the full span of 80 pages, there is a wealth of information supplied concerning the use of *prophētēs* – *most of which deals with the OT and NT uses of the word.* However, Grudem chose to draw from the least relevant section: *profane (secular) Greek,* a section which spans thirteen pages. Moreover, the portion of text from which he derived his list is found in the subsection entitled, *The Broader Use (i.e., uses of the word prophētēs in the broadest realm of the pagan & secular world),* or as Krämer says, "From the earliest examples there may be seen a use of the group[48] which goes beyond anything thus far mentioned."[49] Thus, Krämer's "Broader Use" section is clearly designed to reveal the most extreme and outlier uses of *prophētēs* among secularists and pagans in the Graeco-Roman world. The significance here must not be understated. Being from the state of California, I would like to offer a contemporary analogy that might help the reader to consider the inherent problem with Grudem's method. Specifically, years ago in Southern California (the home of various forms of "valley slang" and other torturous distortions of the English language), the word "righteous" became popular among the youth culture as an expression denoting something as being "cool" (i.e., something was deemed as approved and acceptable by the standard and preferences of man). This is no small transformation of meaning, especially when we consider the foundation of the Bible itself. The scriptural concept of *righteous* and *righteousness* denotes the absolute reality of God being the *right* or *perfect standard* of everything (H. *zādiyk,* G. *dikaios*), yet young people were blurting out the word *righteous* in order to speak of things that were considered as "cool" *by the*

---

[47] The reason why this section is so lengthy is because it relates to the deep background of the word's use from the OT to the LXX and NT.

[48] Group, as in the *word group of prophētēs: prophētēs, prophētis, prophēteuo, prophēteia, prophētikos, pseudoprophētēs.*

[49] Gerhard Kittel, <u>The Theological Dictionary of the New Testament</u>, (Grand Rapids MI: WM. B. Eerdmans Publishing, 1967), 6:793.

subjective standards of men. We would call this use of the term *righteous* the *broader* use of the term from the *secular* realm. As such, it represents a meaning that is the *polar opposite of the historic biblical concept* making its lexical relevance null and void for any serious examination of such a well-defined scriptural term. In a sense, this is what Grudem has done with the word *prophētēs*. By consulting a very thin and extreme portion of pagan history, Grudem has supplied us with an inverted notion of *infallible prophecy: fallible prophecy.* As already mentioned, it isn't very difficult to find outlier examples from the secular or pagan realm – but a tactic such as this doesn't help us to understand the *biblical meanings of biblical words.* When the student of Scripture wishes to understand the use and meaning of biblical words, he must be careful to give priority to the Scriptures themselves to govern his studies, and this includes his lexical analysis of word meanings. After all, no prophecy of Scripture is a matter of one's own interpretation – down to the last sentence, phrase, word, jot, and tittle. The temptation to infuse scriptural words with human "wisdom" (whether secular or pagan) is an ancient one, and it is dangerous:

> 1 Corinthians 2:12–14 — 12 Now we have received, not the spirit of the world, but the Spirit who is from God, so that we may know the things freely given to us by God, 13 which things we also speak, not in words taught by human wisdom, but in those taught by the Spirit, combining spiritual thoughts with spiritual words. 14 But a natural man does not accept the things of the Spirit of God, for they are foolishness to him; and he cannot understand them, because they are spiritually appraised. (NASB95)

Remarkably, there is more. Perhaps unbeknownst to the reader, Grudem's citation of Krämer ends mid-sentence, thereby truncating an important development of thought. Here are further selections from Krämer, before and after Grudem's citation:

Krämer's Article, Preceding Grudem's Citation: Section 4 - Summary (Profane Greek): "Historical seers and prophets not connected with an oracle are never called *prophētai* but *chresmologoi* or the like. On the other hand prophesying demons and gods may be called the *prophētēs* of a higher god as well as men (→ 790, 26 ff.), though it is worth noting that this does not apply to the supreme god Zeus..."[50]

Grudem's Citation: "...Yet, because 'every prophet declares something which is not his own,' the Greek word for 'herald' (*kērux*) 'is the closest synonym,...'"[51]

Krämer's Article, Following Grudem's Citation: "...for the *kērux*, too, declares what he receives from another, > III, 687, 21 ff. This parallelism (> III, 691, 5 ff.) applies also to the occasional function of being a spokesman to the gods > 790, 7.; 792, 7 f.; 794, 1 ff. The prophet occupies a mediatorial role. He is the mouthpiece of the god and he is also man's spokesman to the god."[52]

It certainly would be unfair to expect Grudem to offer the entire article by Krämer, however, just a brief continuation of the original quote reveals much about the section from which he draws, and all of this should remind us of the dangerous import that comes from secular thinking. If we were to entertain Krämer's *broader use* of *prophētēs* for our understanding of a NT prophet, then we would also expect such heralds to speak on behalf of the gods and demons, minus the "supreme god Zeus." As we read further, why not emphasize the need to pray to God through such NT prophets as our intercessory *pontifices*, since such a "prophet" was considered to be *man's spokesman to the god*? Exactly how is it that Grudem can allow himself the freedom and license to draw selectively from such outlier sources, while stopping short of *demonic prophesy* or *human intercession* in prayer as mentioned in Krämer's article? Grudem's lexical analysis is nothing more than a sleight-of-hand

---

[50] Kittel, TDNT, 6:795.
[51] Grudem, Systematic Theology, 1051.
[52] Kittel, TDNT, 6:795.

procedure and those who fail to fact-check his reference work may be inclined to accept his argument at face value – but they do so to their own peril. However, I should remind the reader that Krämer's article is, in fact, helpful but not in the way which Grudem utilizes it. What Krämer reveals in his work shows forth the dark, sad, and confused reality of the 1st century pagan world:

"In Roman (and Greek) religion, the first task was to discover the name of the god whom the worshipper wished to influence and to invoke that name. As Augustine, quoting Varro, who wrote 400 years earlier, puts it: 'We will be able to know what god we should invoke in every circumstance so that we don't behave like comedians who pray for water from Bacchus and for wine from Nymphus.' Given the complicated nature of Roman belief, by which almost every activity was thought to be divinely controlled, it needed considerable ingenuity to be able to choose the appropriate deity when required. It was for this reason that the *pontifices* compiled the elaborate and largely artificial lists of *Indigitamenta*[53] as an exhaustive handbook of invocations for use on every occasion."[54]

Unfortunately, modern day Roman Catholicism has established its religious replicas from the 1st century Roman world. The ancient concept of the intercessory *pontifices* still abides in Rome today beneath the false guise of Christianity – but such pagan constructs have no place within genuine Christianity. The point is simply this: those who substitute biblical definitions with pagan and secular concepts expose themselves and their followers to untold dangers and immeasurable confusion. I should mention at this point that a growing trend in modern scholarship is one that argues that the NT writers were deeply immersed in, and influenced by, intertestamental Jewish writings along with Jewish oral

---

[53] The *Indigitamenta* was an authorized list of deities to whom the *pontifices* (religious intercessors "bridges") prayed. W.H. Roscher's compiled list includes 143 such deities.
[54] Robert Maxwell Ogilvie, <u>The Romans and Their Gods in the age of Augustus</u>, (New York: W W Norton & Company, 1969), 24-25.

THE FALLIBLE PROPHETS OF NEW CALVINISM

traditions as codified within the Mishnah and the Gemara. In mentioning this, I am not presuming to know Mr. Grudem's position on such matters, yet it should be noted that in his most recent version of *The Gift of Prophecy in the New Testament and Today*, Grudem consults such extrabiblical Jewish literature in his effort to suggest that the NT writers had adopted a less authoritative view of a *prophet* – similar to the aforementioned definitions within profane Greek.[55] The subject of extrabiblical Jewish writing is a lengthy one, and I have already written on this subject elsewhere,[56] but I would simply remind the reader that the Savior's own response to such extrabiblical influences was inscripturated for all eternity when He, with great rebuke, said: "You are experts as setting aside the commandment of God *in order to keep your tradition*" (Mark 7:9, italics mine). Simply put, the Apostolic example is the one to emulate, not the Pharisees, especially as we seek to understand core biblical ideas *and words*. If we wish to understand the New Testament prophet's authority, then we need to do so by means of real, scriptural authority. Contrary to Grudem's suppositions, the *biblical writers* were uninfluenced by such extrabiblical and pagan notions of prophecy. In fact, Luke reminds us of the central *priority* and *habit* of the Apostle Paul in Acts 17:2-3:

Acts 17:1–3:   1 Now when they had traveled through Amphipolis and Apollonia, they came to Thessalonica, where there was a synagogue of the Jews. 2 And according to Paul's custom, he went to them, and for three Sabbaths reasoned with them from the Scriptures, 3 explaining and giving evidence that the Christ had to suffer and rise again from the dead, and saying, "This Jesus whom I am proclaiming to you is the Christ."

---

[55] Men like E.P. Sanders and N.T. Wright have helped to accelerate such forms of thinking, and its impact on the church is remarkably destructive.

[56] Michael John Beasley, Indeed, Has Paul Really Said: A Critique of N.T. Wright's Teaching on Justification (Pfafftown NC: The Armoury Ministries, 2010).

The primary[57] verb depicting Paul's didactic habit[58] is the word *reasoned* – (*dielexato*). What modifies this core verb is the prepositional phrase – *from the Scriptures.* This modifying phrase grounds our understanding of the participial modifiers which follow: *explaining* and *giving evidence.* Overall, Paul's reasoning was *from the Scriptures:* this is how he *explained truths* to others, and it contained the very *evidences* which he supplied. Remember, this was Paul's *habit - reasoning from the Scriptures.*[59] This should remind us that Paul was not an *expositor of secular thinking or worldly wisdom.*[60] It should also remind us that when Luke uses the word, *Scriptures,* he is referring to the Old Testament Scriptures since the New Testament canon had not yet been fully brought to completion. The point is simply this: the Old Testament supplied a crucial foundation of thinking concerning the Gospel as it was being revealed to the world in the early stages of the church. It also supplied a crucial record concerning the manner in which God *spoke long ago to the fathers in the prophets in many portions and in many ways.* Thus, important theological *explanations, evidences, and key words* were rooted in such ancient Scripture, providing an important anchor to the New Covenant truths being proclaimed. The harmony of all the Scriptures, both Old and New Testament, is indeed beautiful. After all, *God is not the author of confusion.*[61] However, Grudem's lexical analysis of *prophētēs* supplies a

---

[57] Two main verbs govern verse 2: *1. "he went"* and *2. "he reasoned."* However, our focus is on Paul's instructional habit in particular; but it is important to mention his precious habit of *going to the people who needed to hear the Gospel.* Without the first verb, there would not be the opportunity for the second. This is a central fulfillment of his calling as an *Apostle of Jesus Christ.*

[58] Acts 17:2 And according to Paul's custom [*ethos*]: G. *ethos: to be in the habit of.*

[59] It is important to note that Paul didn't just do this in Thessalonica, but Luke repeats the same verb (reasoned - *dielexato*), when Paul ministered in Athens (Acts 17:17) and in Corinth (Acts 18:4). Clearly, Paul's habit was to exposit and communicate God's word.

[60] 1 Corinthians 2:3-5.

[61] 1 Corinthians 14:33.

profound disharmony between the Old and New Testament definitions of prophecy:

Order	Old Testament	New Testament	"Broader" Profane (secular) uses of the Greek word *prophētēs*; Jewish Extrabiblical Writings
1.		Apostles *(apostolon)*	
2.	Prophets *(BHS: nāḇiy')* *(LXX: prophētēs)*	OT Prophets Moses, Isaiah, etc... *(INFALLIBLE)*	
3.		*Pastors and Teachers*	
4.		"NT Prophets" *(FALLIBLE "Herald")*	FALLIBLE Prophet – herald, philosopher, teacher...

Rather than having a meaningful connection between the Old and New Testament Scriptures, Grudem's imposition of extrabiblical influences produces nothing less than a confused lexical maze. It is also interesting to note that because of this imposition, NT prophecy is seen by him as having less authority than that of a teacher. This lateral comparison of terms reveals one of the core arguments of *fallible prophecy:* a dualistic meaning of the word *prophētēs* in view of a supposed, secularized use of the word by the New Testament writers. In his book, *The Gift of Prophecy in the New Testament and Today*, Grudem argues that only the NT Apostles are "connected" with the Old Testament prophets. This, coupled with his secularized definition of NT prophecy, establishes a conflicted use of the term: *If the genuine prophet is from the Old Testament, then that prophet was infallible; if the genuine prophet is from the New Testament era, then that prophet is fallible.* Thomas Edgar's insights into this problem are especially helpful:

"...Grudem argues that the term *prophet* had come to have a broader connotation in the world of that day, so that it would not carry the idea of 'one sent with absolute divine authority.'...certainly, the word *apostle* had a much broader connotation in Greek culture than the word *prophet*. Why choose an even broader term if this were the problem?...if there were some such problem with the term *prophētēs*, then why did God use it at all and, in particular, why did he use it to refer to the second ranking group in the church? The reason why the apostles are called apostles and not prophets is because they are in fact a special group, the apostles."[62]

Edgar brings up an important point. Grudem's effort to draw a direct and lateral correspondence between OT prophets and NT apostles renders a misleading oversimplification. In Christ was something that was *much greater* than *the temple* (Matt. 12:6), *the prophet Jonah* (Matt. 12:41), *King Solomon* (Matt. 12:42), *and Moses himself* (John 1:17). The apostolic office encompassed many gifts, including prophecy,[63] preaching,[64] and teaching;[65] but it was most centrally distinguished by means of a representative leadership of the church as Christ's immediate envoys. Christ's headship over the church did not end through His ascension, but continued through the unique, apostolic office.[66] When we consider the broad spectrum of Old Testament prophets, nothing directly comports with the apostolic office in the New Testament, especially when we consider this unique component of leadership. The apostles were not OT kings, but they did possess *unique leadership responsibilities* in their representation of the *King of kings and Lord of lords*. I would suggest that there is a better model of comparison between the Old Testament and the New Testament offices, and such a comparison is not lateral, but vertical. In the parable of the rich man and Lazarus, Christ refers to the Old Testament Scriptures as: *Moses and the prophets*.[67] This expression is striking, especially when we recall that Moses too was a prophet who delivered revelation like other prophets;[68] yet Christ distinguished him in

---

[62] Edgar, <u>Satisfied by the Promise of the Spirit</u>, 75-76.

[63] Revelation 1:3.

[64] 1 Timothy 2:7.

[65] 2 Timothy 1:10.

[66] Acts 2:42-43, 4:33-5:12, 6:6, 8:14, 9:27, 15:2-23, 16:4; 1 Cor. 12:28

[67] Luke 16:29-31.

[68] Deut. 34:10.

this special way. Such a distinction is important, especially since Moses, as the Lord's special servant, was the uniquely called leader of the nation of Israel. Moses was not a king, yet He served on behalf of the Lord over all kings, rulers, and nations. Unlike other prophets in the Old Testament, Moses stands out as one who was given unique responsibilities in a way that places him in a special class of God's chosen servants; and yet, *something greater than Moses is here.* Thus, when Christ identified the Old Testament Scriptures as *Moses and the prophets*, this suggests a vertical corollary to the New Testament *apostles and prophets* in the following manner:

N E W	C O V E N A N T	
Christ	**Apostles (infallible)**	**NT Prophets (infallible)**
OT Shadows	**Moses (Leadership /Revelation)**	**...and the prophets (Revelation)**
O L D	C O V E N A N T	

I would submit to the reader that the Scriptures give us a simplicity and beauty of understanding concerning such terms as *apostle* and *prophet,* whereas Grudem's lexical grid should make us wonder how it is that the Old Testament prophets and New Testament teachers can be counted as being greater than New Testament prophets.

Order	New Testament
1.	Apostles *(apostolon)*
2.	OT Prophets Moses, Isaiah, etc... *(INFALLIBLE)*
3.	*Pastors and Teachers*
4.	"NT Prophets" *(FALLIBLE "Herald")*

Other Lexical and Syntactic Concerns

Thus far, our examination of Grudem's definition of a prophet reminds us that even the slightest adjustment of a single word can change entire systems of theology. Grudem's deference towards extrabiblical sources, when defining a word like *prophētes*, is especially problematic. However, with much irony, Grudem elsewhere expresses concern for those who rely on extrabiblical sources when defining biblical terms as in the case of those who consult the *Didache* for their lexical interpretation of New Testament prophecy and the Greek word *diakrinō:*

> "It does not seem helpful to me to appeal to the non-scriptural early writing called the *Didache* to establish a claim to Scripture-quality authority for New Testament congregational prophecies, for the *Didache* simply contradicts Paul on this point (as explained in the text of this book). The *Didache* is not part of the Bible, and I think here and elsewhere it is simply wrong."[69]

Grudem's willingness to consult extrabiblical sources is remarkably selective. When they support his preferred view, he relies upon them with much strength. When they contradict his preferred view, he becomes quite dismissive, reminding us that such sources are not part of the Bible. In the end, no matter what lexical analysis we may pursue, Scripture must always formulate our foundation of thinking, in all contexts, lest we enter into grave error. Grudem's use of extrabiblical sources does not stop with the word *prophētēs.* In this section we will consider the manner in which Grudem handles Agabus' prophetic utterance in Acts 21:11. Similar to his treatment of the word *prophētēs*, leans heavily on extrabiblical sources in order to define Agabus' prophetic claim. Remember that when Agabus delivered his prophecy, he prefaced it as follows:

> "This is what the Holy Spirit says *[tade legei to pneuma to ʽagion]*..." Acts 21:11

Since it is Grudem who has presented Agabus as a crucial example of NT *fallible prophecy*, one must wonder how such an example should be imitated in the modern church according to an accepted interpretation of *fallible prophecy*:

---

[69] Grudem, <u>The Gift of Prophecy</u>, 311.

"So prophecies in the church today should be considered merely human words, not God's words, and not equal to God's words in authority. But does this conclusion conflict with current charismatic teaching or practice? I think it conflicts with much charismatic practice, but not with most charismatic teaching. Most charismatic teachers today would agree that contemporary prophecy is not equal to Scripture in authority. Though some will speak of prophecy as being the 'word of God' for today, there is almost uniform testimony from all sections of the charismatic movement that prophecy is imperfect and impure, and will contain elements that are not to be obeyed or trusted. For example, Bruce Yocum, the author of a widely used charismatic book on prophecy, writes, 'Prophecy can be impure-our thoughts, or ideas can get mixed into the message we receive – whether we receive the words directly or only receive a sense of the message.' But it must be said that in actual practice much confusion results from the habit of prefacing prophecies with the common Old Testament phrase, 'Thus says the Lord' (a phrase nowhere spoken in the New Testament by any prophets in New Testament churches). This is unfortunate, because it gives the impression that the words that follow are God's very words, whereas the New Testament does not justify that position and, when pressed, most responsible charismatic spokesmen would not want to claim it for every part of their prophecies anyway. So there would be much gain and no loss if that introductory phrase were dropped. Now it is true that Agabus uses a similar phrase ("Thus says the Holy Spirit") in Acts 21:11, but the same words (Gk. *Tade legei*) are used by Christian writers just after the time of the New Testament to introduce very general paraphrases or greatly expanded interpretations of what is being reported (so Ignatius, *Epistle to the Philadelphians* 7:1-2 [about A.D. 108] and *Epistle of Barnabas* 6:8, 9:2, 5 [A.D. 70-100]). The phrase can apparently mean, 'This is generally (or approximately) what the Holy Spirit is saying to us.'"[70]

This paragraph alone reveals the abundance of confusion that comes when one tries to infuse the label *"prophet"* with a foreign notion of

---

[70] Ibid., 1055-56.

legitimate[71] *fallibility.* The inherent dualism of this doctrine shows forth the divided results that it will produce for those who embrace it. If someone claims to reveal a directed message from the Holy Spirit, and yet their "directed" utterance cannot be trusted as if given by the Holy Spirit, then why should the church be encouraged to refer to such a person as *a prophet of God*, especially in view of the historic, biblical understanding of the term? Can it really be said that God sends forth prophets who speak thus? Is this the kind of thinking that we should harbor concerning the true God, or is it not the machination of ancient paganism? Grudem's attempt to reconcile the irreconcilable is even more striking when he mentions Agabus in this section. Look again at the immediate context of Grudem's treatment of Agabus:

> "Now it is true that Agabus uses a similar phrase ("Thus says the Holy Spirit") in Acts 21:11, but the same words (Gk. *Tade legei*) are used by Christian writers just after the time of the New Testament to introduce very general paraphrases or greatly expanded interpretations of what is being reported (so Ignatius, Epistle to the Philadelphians 7:1-2 [about A.D. 108] and Epistle of Barnabas 6:8, 9:2, 5 [A.D. 70-100]). The phrase can apparently mean, 'This is generally (or approximately) what the Holy Spirit is saying to us.'"[72]

Please do not miss Grudem's sleight-of–hand approach to Agabus' expression, *"Thus says the Holy Spirit"* (in the NASB, *"this is what the Holy Spirit says"*). Grudem sidelines Agabus' attribution to the Holy Spirit, garnering only a slender portion of his expression (*tade legei*). Then, forgoing scriptural parallels to Agabus' broader statement, Grudem consults extrabiblical sources in his quest to define *tade legei*. The

---

[71] Grudem's innovations have made it necessary to generate hyphenated expressions when referring to his brand of NT prophecy. I use the word *legitimate* in order to recognize that Grudem's invented category nearly eliminates the concept of a false prophet, since *fallibility* is presumed to be an accepted component to the contemporary utterances given by a supposed "NT fallible-prophet."

[72] Ibid., 1056.

illegitimacy of this method strains the imagination. If we want to scrutinize Agabus' attribution of his prophecy, *"Thus says the Holy Spirit [tade legei to pneuma to 'agion]"* or a similar expression giving attribution to the Holy Spirit, [*legei to pneuma*], then it behooves us to look for *correlative* examples in Scripture in order to inspect how they were used and applied in their own context. Normally, an exegete *of Scripture* would offer parallel examples *from the Bible* in order to discern the meaning and intent of such an expression. But Grudem deflects us from the expression at hand *[tade legei to pneuma to 'agion]* and sends us searching in the extrabiblical works of Ignatius and Barnabas. Which leads me to the following observation: one finds much that is disconcerting in what Grudem writes, however, there is equal concern over what he *doesn't write*. For example, if I as an engineer informed you that the bridge that you are about to travel over is reliable and safe based upon the fact that the structure in question has passed most of its safety inspections, then you might feel confident to proceed forward. What I haven't told you is that the same bridge actually failed 49% of its inspections. To a discerning driver, such an omission is no small matter, the revelation of which would likely change one's driving plans. It is in this sense that I express amazement over what it is that Grudem selectively withholds from the reader. The aforementioned example of Grudem's selective quotation from TDNT underscores my point, but his omission of scriptural parallels to Agabus' *"this is what the Holy Spirit says [tade legei to pneuma to 'agion]"* further expands it. Therefore, let us consult the more relevant, biblical parallels concerning our text in queston:

- **Acts 21:11:** And coming to us, he took Paul's belt and bound his own feet and hands, and said, *"This is what the Holy Spirit says [tade legei[73] to pneuma to 'agion]:* 'In this way the Jews at Jerusalem will bind the man who owns this belt and deliver him into the hands of the Gentiles.' "* In all

---

[73] 3rd person singular, present active indicative of *legō*.

of the parallels supplied below, the reader should note the *arthrous* use of the word *pneuma* which is rightly translated as *the Spirit,* i.e. *the Spirit of God.* In Acts 21:11 and Hebrews 3:7, we have the addition of *to ʼagion,* i.e., *the Holy* Spirit. These examples align themselves most closely with Acts 21:11, and in every case, the question of *indicative*[74] *attribution* is quite clear. It is *the Spirit* of God who speaks with *indicative certainty,* delivering the revelation of God Himself:

- **Acts 8:29:** *"the Spirit said [eipen*[75] *de to pneuma]* to Philip, 'Go up and join this chariot...'"* This revelation from God was given in reference to Philip's needed ministry to the Ethiopian eunuch. Philip rightly obeyed this declaration of the Lord.

- **Acts 13:2:** Luke records for us what the Spirit revealed concerning Paul and Barnabas, *"...the Holy Spirit said [eipen*[76] *to pneuma to ʼagion],* 'Set apart for Me Barnabas and Saul for the work to which I have called them'"* (Acts 13:2). Once again, like Paul and his companions in Acts 21, we find submission and obedience to the will of the Lord.

- **Hebrews 3:7:** Outside of the book of Acts, we have yet another, unmistakable parallel in Hebrews — 7 Therefore, just as *the Holy Spirit says [kathos legei to pneuma to ʼagion],* "Today if you hear His voice, 8 Do not harden your hearts as when they provoked Me, As in the day of trial in the wilderness, 9 Where your fathers tried Me by testing Me, And saw My works for forty years. 10 "Therefore I was angry with this generation, And said, 'They always go astray in their heart, And they did not know My ways'; 11 As I swore in My wrath, 'They shall not enter My rest.'"[77]

---

[74] An indicative verb denotes reality, not mere possibility or potentiality.

[75] 3rd person singular, aorist active indicative, irregular verb form of *lego.*

[76] 3rd person singular, aorist active indicative, irregular verb form of *lego.*

[77] The author of Hebrews quotes from the Old Testament from verse 7b through 11 of chapter 3. In verse 7, he cites *what the Spirit said* in Psalm 95.

- **Revelation 2:7:** John was commissioned by the Lord to record the book of revelation for the church and her posterity: "write in a book what you see, and send it to the seven churches." In view of this, it is no wonder that the same expression appears in view of the Spirit's activity of direct revelation: **2:7** 'He who has an ear, let him hear what *the Spirit says [to pneuma legei]* to the churches. To him who overcomes, I will grant to eat of the tree of life which is in the Paradise of God.' **Revelation 14:13:** And I heard a voice from heaven, saying, "Write, 'Blessed are the dead who die in the Lord from now on!' " "Yes," *says the Spirit [legei to pneuma],* "so that they may rest from their labors, for their deeds follow with them."

In each of these examples, every use of the verb *legō* is in the indicative voice, denoting direct and real action. Thus, there is no sense in which we could say that the Spirit "might be indicating" or is "possibly saying" etc. No, the root nature of an indicative verb points to absolute reality. In fact, Grudem's own tactic of focusing exclusively on the words *tade legei* fails to support his connotation of "the Spirit might be indicating" or is "possibly saying." The seriousness of this failure is evident in Christ's own use of this expression:

Revelation 2:1, 8, 12, 18; 3:1, 7, 14 [*tade legei*]: In the book of Revelation, Christ charges the apostle John to write seven letters (Ephesus, Smyrna, Pergamum, Thyatira, Sardis, Philadelphia, and Laodicea), all of which are prefaced with the authoritative, *indicative* expression: *tade legei.*

The question of indicative attribution in all of these examples is quite plain and clear: in each case, it is the Lord God who speaks to His people, supplying divine and infallible revelation, not the words of men. By contrast, parallels such as these would make Agabus' claim all the more odd if in fact he spoke in error when prophesying. The fact that Grudem avoids these important passages in his *Systematic Theology*, while sending his readers on the rabbit trail of extrabiblical sources, is simply stunning. All of this combined makes his concluding interpretation of Agabus' expression, *"this is what the Holy Spirit says,"* all the more incredible. Consider, once more, what he says about this as cited earlier:

> "The phrase can apparently mean, 'This is generally (or approximately) what the Holy Spirit is saying to us.' If someone really does think God is bringing something to mind which should be reported in the congregation, there is nothing wrong with saying *'I think the Lord is putting on my mind that...'* or *'It seems to me that the Lord is showing us...'* or some similar expression."[78]

Grudem never offers an adequate explanation of Agabus' expression, *"this is what the Holy Spirit says."* Perhaps we might infer from his teaching that the expression, "this is what the Holy Spirit says," actually means: "'This is generally (or approximately) what the Holy Spirit is saying to us'" or "'I think the Lord is putting on my mind that...' or 'It seems to me that the Lord is showing us...'" But one must wonder, if Grudem thinks that it is inappropriate and unhelpful for New Testament prophets to invoke the expression, *thus says the Lord,* would he then find it acceptable if someone were to stand and say, *this is what the Holy Spirit says – with such direct and indicative attribution?* After all, if we have in Scripture Agabus as an example of a New Testament fallible prophet, then wouldn't he be a helpful model for the supposed *fallible prophets* of the modern day? Along with this, if the expression, *this is what the Holy Spirit says* approximates the expression: *this is generally (or approximately) what the Holy Spirit is saying to us,* then how should the interpreter read and decipher passages like Hebrews 3:7, Revelation 2:7, 14:13, or Acts 8:29 and 13:2; or even Christ's epistles to the seven churches in the book of Revelation? Moreover, would Grudem have us to believe that the author of Hebrews sees his cited text of Ps 95:7-11 as being *"approximately"* what the Holy Spirit is saying? Such a duality of thinking is nothing less than an outright contradiction, lending itself to other potentially dangerous teachings.

---

[78] Grudem, <u>Systematic Theology</u>, 1056.

Though we are not entirely finished with our study of the word prophet, I wanted to expose the reader to the lexical reasoning for *fallible prophecy* as supplied by Wayne Grudem. Having done so, we must press on to the example of Agabus, whose example is central to the proponents of *fallible prophecy*. Much has been written on this matter, and Grudem has already responded to several of his critics. Therefore, it is not my intention to repeat what has already been written thus far, rather, I hope to offer a more thorough examination of the subject especially in view of some questions and observations that have not yet been fully addressed.

As we press on to the story of Agabus, we must consider what is inherited through his example, – as interpreted by the theology of *fallible prophecy.*

CHAPTER 3:

– FALLIBLE PROPHECY –

THE CASE OF AGABUS

Thus far, we have considered the serious nature of the prophetic office as revealed in the Old Testament Scriptures. It is no exaggeration to say that those who claimed to be a prophet were making a life or death decision, and it was the responsibility of God's people to evaluate such a claim by the standards of God's prescribed tests. Then, in the previous chapter, we moved forward with an analysis of the New Testament writers' use of the word *prophētēs*. Within this discussion, we considered the troubling import of Grudem's extrabiblical lexical analysis of such a historic word. Grudem's modifications of the word *prophecy* are not minor, but are instead systemic seeing that he has effectively reversed the connotation of *infallible prophecy* to its polar opposite: *fallible prophecy*. What is so remarkable about Grudem's argumentative effort is his blatant willingness to infuse the term *prophet* with extreme, outlier connotations of profane (secular) Greek ideals. In many respects, such an argumentative procedure reveals a lack of real substance by the advocates of *fallible prophecy,* as Thomas Edgar has noted:

> "The seemingly endless series of tenuous and indirect arguments is due to the fact that there are no direct statements of Scripture to support the 'fallible prophet' concept."[79]

Edgar's observation deserves further consideration. Since the proponents of *fallible prophecy* are the ones arguing for a complete redefinition of the term *prophet*, a very heavy burden of proof rests upon their shoulders. If the New Testament really does demand a radical transformation of such an ancient Old Testament concept, then we should expect to find clear and cogent examples of *fallible prophecy* in the New Testament Scriptures. Thus, if New Testament prophets really were *fallible, while being accepted as legitimate messengers,* then we should expect to see evidences for this: some *implicit* and others *explicit*. Grudem believes that the Scriptures supply both *implicit* and *explicit* proofs of such *accepted*

---

[79] Edgar, <u>Satisfied by the Promise</u>, 80.

fallibility. His *implicit* arguments rely mostly on his interpretation of 1 Corinthians 14:5, 29 and 1 Thessalonians 5:19-21 (which will be examined more thoroughly in the next chapter), while his *explicit* proof of *fallible prophecy* rests most heavily on his interpretation of the prophecy of Agabus. Only in Agabus do we have the historian Luke identifying a *prophet who actually prophesied*. His example plays a central role to the thinking of *fallible prophecy* since it is argued that he was partially right and partially wrong when he uttered his prophecy in Acts 21. It is this notion of an admixture of error and truth that is central to the idea of the New Testament fallible prophet. In such a paradigm as this, believers are enjoined to "sift the good from the bad, accepting some and rejecting the rest"[80] by the advice of Grudem and others. Agabus' prophecy is simple enough, yet the real complexity comes when one considers the manner in which it was fulfilled:

> Acts 21:11: And coming to us, he took Paul's belt and bound his own feet and hands, and said, "This is what the Holy Spirit says: 'In this way the Jews at Jerusalem will bind the man who owns this belt and deliver him into the hands of the Gentiles.'"

According to Grudem and others, Agabus was right about Paul being arrested in Jerusalem, yet wrong about the manner in which this would take place:

> "He would have the general idea correct (Paul would be imprisoned at Jerusalem), but the details somewhat wrong."[81]

> Agabus' prophecies of "...'binding' and 'giving over' by the Jews—are explicitly falsified by the subsequent narrative"[82]

---

[80] Grudem, Systematic Theology, 1054.

[81] Grudem, The Gift of Prophecy, 81.

[82] Ibid., 80.

D.A. Carson is more direct in his accusations of the New Testament prophet:

"I can think of no reported Old Testament prophet whose prophecies are so wrong on the details."[83]

Grudem goes so far in his judgment of Agabus, that he places his prophecy beneath the condemnation of Deuteronomy 18:22:

"I find it hard to reconcile with the Old Testament pattern of precise fulfillment of prophecies (strictly speaking, Agabus predicted two events which 'did not come to pass,' Deut. 18:22)..."[84]

"...by Old Testament standards, Agabus would have been condemned as a false prophet, because in Acts 21:27-35 neither of his predictions are fulfilled."[85]

We have already covered the seriousness of charging a prophet with the guilt of *presumption (H. ziyd),* and I would suggest to the reader that we should have far more evidence before doing so. Apart from any *explicit* evidence, it is a very grave matter to accuse Agabus of error or presumption. Moreover, I believe that Thomas is right when he says:

"He is accusing not only Agabus of error, Grudem is making the same accusation against the Holy Spirit."[86]

If Grudem is wrong about *fallible prophecy,* then he is very seriously wrong. Without clear and explicit proof of error or presumption, we should be far more guarded about rendering such accusations against a prophet of God. As mentioned earlier, extensive critiques of Grudem's

[83] Ibid.
[84] Ibid., 81-82.
[85] Ibid., 79.
[86] Thomas, Prophecy Rediscovered?, 91.

views have been written by Thomas, Edgar, Farnell, and Compton, however, there are dimensions of the *fallible prophecy* debate that still require a more thorough analysis. Because of this it is my hope to provide the reader with some new observations concerning Agabus' prophecy and how his example raises further concerns about the clarity and efficacy of *fallible prophecy*. As we proceed with the subject of Agabus it is important to remember that his prophecy encompasses only one verse (Acts 21:11); however, in order to scrutinize the question of his prophecy's fulfillment (or lack thereof), we will need to examine a significant span of passages, specifically Acts 21:11-23:22. Additionally, there are corroborating passages that we will also need to consult in Acts chapters 24-26 and 28. In light of the sheer volume of requisite texts for this subject, it is no surprise that Agabus' example is not a simple one. Let us consider Agabus' prophecy once again, but in a wider context of Luke's narrative:

> Acts 21:10–14 — 10 As we were staying there for some days, a prophet named Agabus came down from Judea. 11 And coming to us, he took Paul's belt and bound his own feet and hands, and said, "This is what the Holy Spirit says: 'In this way the Jews at Jerusalem will bind the man who owns this belt and deliver him into the hands of the Gentiles.' " 12 When we had heard this, we as well as the local residents began begging him not to go up to Jerusalem. 13 Then Paul answered, "What are you doing, weeping and breaking my heart? For I am ready not only to be bound, but even to die at Jerusalem for the name of the Lord Jesus." 14 And since he would not be persuaded, we fell silent, remarking, "The will of the Lord be done!" (NASB95)

Acts 21:10-14 brings us to a very important turning point in Paul's life. It is here that we see the apostle entering into a new stage of suffering and ministry for the sake of the Gospel, from Jerusalem to Rome. In many respects, Agabus' prophecy introduces us to that which Christ already revealed concerning Paul's calling as an apostle to the Gentiles:

Acts 9:15–16 — 15 But the Lord said to him, "Go, for he is a chosen instrument of Mine, to bear My name before the Gentiles and kings and the sons of Israel; 16 for I will show him how much he must suffer for My name's sake." (NASB95)

The Savior revealed, from the beginning, that Paul would not only preach the Gospel to Jewish and Gentile populations at large, *but even to kings.* This mystery of how Paul would be enabled to proclaim truth to monarchs is not unveiled until we enter into the narrative of Acts chapter 21, and the prophecy of Agabus is an important portal through which we begin to see such a reality. As we read through Acts 21-28 it becomes quite clear that Paul's seizure by the Romans was the instrumental means by which Christ would dispatch His chosen instrument to leaders in Caesarea and to the capital of Imperial Rome itself, such that one day, Paul could write to the brethren at Philippi, saying, "All the saints greet you, especially those of *Caesar's household.*" This broader view of Agabus' prophecy is important and helpful, yet we will need to proceed with the more detailed analysis of its fulfillment. Grudem's approach to Agabus is one which rests mostly on the historical narrative of Acts 21:27-36. In summary, it is in this section that we see "all the city" of Jerusalem being "provoked" by Paul's presence and ministry such that he was arrested by the Jews who sought to kill him.[87] Roman soldiers then intervened, arrested, bound, and brought Paul back to the barracks for questioning. With this, Grudem and others insist that Agabus failed in his prophecy concerning Paul being *bound* and *given over* by the Jews. Because of this judgment, Agabus is seen as an example of a New Testament *fallible prophet. Fallible prophecy* has placed Agabus on trial with a degree of scrutiny never before seen in the history of the church, yet, there remain some unanswered questions within the overall debate. Because of this, we

---

[87] Acts 24:6–7: 6 "And he even tried to desecrate the temple; and then we arrested him. [We wanted to judge him according to our own Law. 7 "But Lysias the commander came along, and with much violence took him out of our hands..."

must be thorough in our analysis. To do this, we will approach our study in three key phases: First, we will review some *historical background* relevant to our study of Paul's arrest as predicted by Agabus. Second, we will examine *three views* of Agabus' use of the word *paradidōmi* that have emerged from the *fallible prophecy* debate over the years. Third, we will consider several *practical implications* that emerge from the doctrine of fallible prophecy.

Historical Background of Paul's Arrest

In this section, we will need to consider several historical contexts relating to Paul's arrest in Jerusalem: *1. Paul's legal status while in Jerusalem; 2. The historical realities of 1ˢᵗ century Roman jurisprudence; 3. Paul's initial arrest in Jerusalem.* These points of analysis will be foundational to our study of Agabus. As we examine the biblical record of Agabus and his prophecy, we must remember that when the people of God seek to evaluate a prophet and his prophecy, such an evaluation is to be pursued out of a love for God;[88] after all, the Lord and His pure word is worth such effort, and so much more:

1. Background - Paul's Legal Status While in Jerusalem: Though Acts 21:27-36 reveals the context of Paul's Roman arrest, it does not give us the full reality of his legal proceedings prior to his transfer from Jerusalem to Caesarea and finally to capitol of Rome itself. Thus, if we really wish to scrutinize Agabus' prophecy carefully then it behooves us to examine the most important stages of Paul's *arrest, self-defense, and interaction with his accusers.* For such a context as this, we will examine four main events within Acts 21:27-23:10:

---

[88] Deuteronomy 13:1-5.

Paul's Seizure[89] and Arrest by the Jews: Acts 21:27–36 — 27 When the seven days were almost over, the Jews from Asia, upon seeing him in the temple, began to stir up all the crowd and laid hands on him, 28 crying out, "Men of Israel, come to our aid! This is the man who preaches to all men everywhere against our people and the Law and this place; and besides he has even brought Greeks into the temple and has defiled this holy place." 29 For they had previously seen Trophimus the Ephesian in the city with him, and they supposed that Paul had brought him into the temple. 30 Then all the city was provoked, and the people rushed together, and taking hold of Paul they dragged him out of the temple, and immediately the doors were shut. 31 While they were seeking to kill him, a report came up to the commander of the Roman cohort that all Jerusalem was in confusion.

Paul's 1st Seizure and Arrest by the Romans - Acts 21:32-36: 32 At once he took along some soldiers and centurions and ran down to them; and when they saw the commander and the soldiers, they stopped beating Paul. 33 Then the commander came up and took hold of him, and ordered him to be bound with two chains; and he began asking who he was and what he had done. 34 But among the crowd some were shouting one thing and some another, and when he could not find out the facts because of the uproar, he ordered him to be brought into the barracks. 35 When he got to the stairs, he was carried by the soldiers because of the violence of the mob; 36 for the multitude of the people kept following them, shouting, "Away with him!" (NASB95)

Paul's 1st Attempted Testimony and 2nd Seizure by the Romans - Acts 21:40-22:22–25: 40 When he had given him permission, Paul, standing on the stairs, motioned to the people with his hand; and when there was a great hush, he spoke to them in the Hebrew dialect, saying,...22 They listened to him up to this statement, and then they raised their voices and said, "Away with such a fellow from the earth, for he should not be allowed to live!" 23 And as they

---

[89] The word *seizure* is here employed in order to acknowledge the manner in which Paul was taken, first by the Jews, then by the Romans. Following Paul's Roman arrest, he was *taken and removed* from public view by the Romans a total of three times. Luke's description of all of these *seizures* occur as follows: 1. Acts 21:30 [*epilabomenoi...eilkon*], 2. Acts 21:34 [*agesthai*], 3. Acts 22:24 [*eisagesthai*], 4. Acts 23:10 [*arpasai*].

were crying out and throwing off their cloaks and tossing dust into the air, 24 the commander ordered him to be brought into the barracks, stating that he should be examined by scourging so that he might find out the reason why they were shouting against him that way. 25 But when they stretched him out with thongs, Paul said to the centurion who was standing by, "Is it lawful for you to scourge a man who is a Roman and uncondemned?"

Paul's 2nd Attempted Testimony and 3rd Seizure by the Romans - Acts 22:30; 23:9-10: 30 But on the next day, wishing to know for certain why he had been accused by the Jews, he released him and ordered the chief priests and all the Council to assemble, and brought Paul down and set him before them...23:9 And there occurred a great uproar; and some of the scribes of the Pharisaic party stood up and began to argue heatedly, saying, "We find nothing wrong with this man; suppose a spirit or an angel has spoken to him?" 10 And as a great dissension was developing, the commander was afraid Paul would be torn to pieces by them and ordered the troops to go down and take him away from them by force, and bring him into the barracks.

The amount of activity that takes place while Paul was in Jerusalem is fairly extensive, and the contexts of his four seizures all vary, yet what we must remember is that once Paul was taken from the Jews in Acts 21:33, he was under Roman custody for the remainder of his time in Jerusalem. Overall, if we are going to examine the question of the fulfillment of Agabus' prophecy, then we must consider the full span of Paul's experiences while he was in Jerusalem.

2. Background - The Historical Realities of 1st Century Roman Jurisprudence: Paul's arrest in Jerusalem brings us to some very important realities concerning Roman law in the 1st century. The Jews' mission to kill Paul would have been very complex in view of the oppressive presence of Roman authority. The Jews would have lived with the daily reminder of this in view of a prominent structure called the Antonia Fortress, built by Herod the Great in the 19 B.C., and located at the northwest corner of the colonnades surrounding the temple courtyard. Josephus indicates that in this structure "there always lay...a Roman legion,"[90] and that the tower of Antonia stood as a "guard to the temple" from which "the whole temple might be viewed...in order to watch the people." [91] It is difficult for modern minds to comprehend the oppressive nature of Rome's oversight in this regard, but if one could imagine annexing a police watchtower and station to a contemporary church building, then a clearer picture might emerge regarding what life was like for the 1st century Jewish worshipper. Luke's mention of this fortress is evident when he indicates that Paul was carried up "the stairs" and into "the barracks" of the Roman soldiers (Acts 21:35-37).[92] All of this reminds us of the fact that the Jews could not carry on their temple worship and activities apart from the watchful eye, oversight, and permission of the Romans; and though the Jews occasionally entertained

---

[90] In Acts 21:31, we first learn about "the command of the Roman *cohort.*" In this example the NASB translators used the word cohort for the Greek word *chiliarchos:* "a military officer, normally in command of a thousand soldiers" Louw, J. P., & Nida, E. A. (1996). Vol. 1: Greek-English lexicon of the New Testament: Based on semantic domains (electronic ed. of the 2nd edition.) (549). New York: United Bible Societies.

[91] "...the entire structure resembled that of a tower, it contained also four other distinct towers at its four corners; whereof the others were but fifty cubits high; whereas that which lay upon the southeast corner was seventy cubits high, that from thence the whole temple might be viewed; (243) but on the corner where it joined to the two cloisters of the temple, it had passages down to them both, through which the guard (244) (for there always lay in this tower a Roman legion) went several ways among the cloisters, with their arms, on the Jewish festivals, in order to watch the people, that they might not there attempt to make any innovations; (245) for the temple was a fortress that guarded the city, as was the tower of Antonia a guard to the temple; and in that tower were the guards of those three." Josephus, F., & Whiston, W. (1987). *The works of Josephus: Complete and unabridged.* Peabody: Hendrickson.

[92] "Paul was in more danger in the midst of the Jews than he was in a Roman prison. So again he was brought up the steps to the army barracks at the Antonia Fortress (cf. 21:35)." Toussaint, S. D. (1985). Acts. In J. F. Walvoord & R. B. Zuck (Eds.), The Bible Knowledge Commentary: An Exposition of the Scriptures (J. F. Walvoord & R. B. Zuck, Ed.) (Ac 23:10). Wheaton, IL: Victor Books.

delusions of freedom,[93] the ominous shadow of the Antonia Fortress reminded them that this was in fact a delusion. Thus, when the Jews attempted to kill Paul themselves, their murderous agenda was utterly obliterated by the overwhelming force of the Roman authorities who quickly rushed on the scene. This initial conflict over Paul is important, especially since it relates to the matter of Roman jurisprudence. Luke tells us that "all the city was provoked, and the people rushed together" (v. 30) and "...a report came up to the commander of the Roman cohort that all Jerusalem was in confusion" (v. 31). These truths meant that there was a great potential for trouble for the mob, Paul, and even the local Roman authorities had the conflict remained unresolved. Paul was most disadvantaged seeing that Judaism was considered a *Religio licita* (a legal religion), while Christianity was not. Such an incident as this could not be laid to rest by the Roman officials, especially if the instigator of the riot was not properly identified, secured, and punished.[94] To be charged with instigating a riot was no small matter in their day. Rome's ancient laws dealing with riotous conduct made it so that anyone who instigated a riot could be liable for property damage, personal injury, or even be found guilty of treason, *depending on the circumstances*. The reality of Rome's regulations regarding any destructive "mob" are summarized by the historian, Justinian:

"If a man on arrival excites a crowd and incites it to an unlawful object by his shouts or by any act such as making accusations against someone or even by arousing pity, and if damage is committed as a result of his malicious

---

[93] John 8:33.

[94] Rome's longstanding history of establishing laws against mob riots and rebellion can be seen in the ancient standard of *Senatus Consultum de re Publica Defendenda* (Decree of the Senate on defending the Republic). This law was first passed in 121 BC in order to quell riotous mobs which formed as a consequence to Gaius Gracchus' fall from power. Throughout its history, Rome applied austere anti-riot laws that sought to quell rebellious uprisings and thereby preserve governmental rule.

incitement, [95] he will be liable, even if he did not originally have the intent of getting the crowd together...when a person gathers a crowd together himself and beats a slave in front of the crowd in order to do him an unlawful injury rather than with intent to cause loss, the Edict will apply."[96]

In all of this we can see that the fear expressed by the town clerk at Ephesus over the riotous mob that had assembled against Paul was quite real and grave:

Acts 19:40 "...indeed we are in danger of being accused of a riot in connection with today's events, since there is no real cause for it, and in this connection we will be unable to account for this disorderly gathering."

Thus, when Luke mentions that *all the city of Jerusalem was provoked,*[97] this meant that a specific set of legal standards came into play automatically.[98] The Jews did not have the final authority to carry out an execution since Jewish civil law was subject to Roman rule. They could seek a formal charge of capital punishment before the council of the Sanhedrin, but once such a judgment was concluded, further steps would have to be taken within the realm of Roman jurisprudence in order for

---

[95] Justinian, The Digest of Roman Law: Theft, Rapine, Damage, and Insult (Middlesex England: Penguin Books, 1979), 157.

[96] In Justinian's *Digest of Roman Law,* we further see the breadth of Rome's anti-riot laws. Not only was the instigator of a mob to be held accountable for his actions, but also the members of the mob themselves are too. Additionally, the law allowed for the prosecution of those who would provoke a crowd by means of "his cries, inflammatory language, or because he aroused pity. Here he is liable even though someone else assembled the mob, because he himself was part of it." Justinian, Digest, 155-156.

[97] Acts 21:30: G. *sundrome* – a riotous gathering.

[98] "...the term 'crowd' means any sort of riotous assembly and that it is derived from the Greek word for making a tumult. How many, then, do we agree make a 'crowd'? If two people are quarrelling we shall not accept them as constituting a crowd, for two people cannot reasonably be said to make any sort of mob. However, if there are more, say ten or fifteen men, they can be called a crowd." Justinian, Digest, 155.

such a penalty to be carried out *legally*.[99] Simply put, the notion of killing Paul was complicated, and those complications increased exponentially as soon as Roman intervention entered the scene and controlled the situation.

3. Background - Paul's Arrest by the Jews: When we consider Paul's initial arrest by the Jews, Luke tells us nothing about how Paul was restrained, except that the Jews *took hold of Paul and dragged him.* Additionally, it is helpful to note that the Jewish attorney, Tertullus, testified before Felix that Paul had been *arrested [ekratēsamen]*[100] because he "stirs up dissension among all the Jews through the world."[101] When we consider this account, we should note that the concept of Paul's arrest by the Jews raises further questions about the manner in which he was restrained by them seeing that the concept of being *formally arrested* typically included the idea of being *bound*, as in the case of John the Baptist and Christ:

---

[99] Of course, the Jews submitted to Roman rule selectively, since they did not cease from executing Stephen when he appeared before the council of the Sanhedrin. Under normal circumstances however, a *formal charge* of capital punishment had to be delivered by the judgment of the council of the Sanhedrin: Sanhedrin 7:1 A "Four modes of execution were given over *to the court* [in order of severity]:" B "(1) stoning, (2) burning, (3) decapitation, and (4) strangulation." Neusner, J. (1988). The Mishnah : A new translation (595–596). New Haven, CT: Yale University Press. Italics mine.

[100] Acts 24:6 G. *ekratēsamen* > *krateō:* Aorist active indicative of.

[101] This should remind us of the force of Rome's ancient anti-riot laws. Such laws made it so that anyone who was thus accused could be liable for property damage, personal injury, or even be found guilty of treason, depending on the circumstances. Thus, Turtullus' appeal to Felix reveals his understanding of Rome's standards against those who instigated mobs. This is very similar to the transformation of testimony that took place with Christ. The Jews' complaint is really doctrinal, but in order to seek an execution *via* Roman authority, other charges were sought.

John the Bapsist: Matthew 14:3 For when Herod had John arrested [*kratēsas*],[102] he bound [*edēsen*][103] him and put him in prison because of Herodias, the wife of his brother Philip. (NASB95)

Jesus Christ: John 18:12 So the Roman cohort and the commander and the officers of the Jews, arrested Jesus and bound [*edēsan*][104] Him, (NASB95)

Though none of this *explicitly* proves that the Jews temporarily bound Paul directly, *it does raise serious questions about the veracity of those who insist that such a matter is impossible.* Despite this, Grudem insists that Paul was never directly bound by the Jews. It would be one thing if Grudem dismissed this discussion for a lack of scriptural evidence, but this has not been his approach. Instead, his argument rests on the absence of any explicit reference to the Jews binding Paul.[105] By rendering an argument which rests on the absence of data, Grudem supplies nothing more than an *argument from ignorance.* To his mind, the fact that Luke says nothing about Paul being *directly* bound by the Jews actually *proves that it never actually occurred.* In reality, the lack of such a record proves nothing by itself.[106]

---

[102] G. *kratēsas* > *krateō:* This is the same word used by Tertullus in Acts 24:3 referring to Paul's "arrest" by the Jews.

[103] G. *edesem* – 3ps aorist active indicative of *deō;* Acts 21:11 – *desousin* – 3pp future active indicative of *deō.*

[104] G. *edesan* – 3pp, aorist active indicative of *deō.*

[105] In this work, we have moved to the debate of Agabus while moving past further questions about the prophetesses of Philip, or the disciples of Tyre. It should be noted that our argument does not rest in the absence of detail about these individuals. In fact, so little is said about these individuals that it becomes difficult to extrapolate from Luke's narratives about them. Thus, it is important to distinguish between an *argument that is derived from ignorance,* versus an *argument that is derived from explicit revelation.* Our agenda is the latter rather than the former.

[106] *Argumentum Ad Ignorantiam:* e.g., Luke does not say that Paul was bound by the Jews; *therefore,* he was not bound by them.

As to the question of Agabus being *bound* by the Jews directly, we can admit that there is no explicit statement in Luke's narrative indicating that he was thus bound. However, the fact that the Jews formally arrested Paul leaves this open as a significant possibility. Overall, Grudem cannot say that it is an impossibility. This is one of the great problems surrounding the *fallible prophecy* debate. Their burden of proof is quite high since they are seeking to prove their case on the basis of an absence of scriptural data. This is very different from one who says, *it is a possibility that Paul was bound by the Jews – even a probability, but it cannot be proven beyond a shadow of a doubt.* This distinction is important since the advocates of *fallible prophecy* are looking to prove, beyond a doubt, that Agabus failed in his prophecy. To do so, they should have much more than an *argument from ignorance.* Yet we must not rest our arguments on what is not in the text of Scripture. If we wish to be cautious about this important matter, we must continue exploring Agabus' prophecy more thoroughly. If we were to assume that Paul was *not directly bound by the Jews* (not by argumentative necessity, but by hypothesis), an alternative view would be that Paul was bound, *instrumentally*, by the Romans. This view has already been proposed by Thomas and others, and Grudem has already offered critical responses to such a view. As well, concerning the question of Paul being *delivered over (paradidōmi)* to the Gentiles, there are three main views that have emerged over the years:

Three Main Views of paradidōmi

Three mains views of Agabus' use of the term *paradidōmi* will be examined in this section addressing the manner in which Paul was *delivered over to the Gentiles*: 1. Paul was *delivered over* to his captors *despite the will of the Jewish mob.* 2. Paul was *delivered over* to his captors *by legal compulsion.* 3. Paul was *willingly delivered over* by the Jews in the face of *Roman jurisprudence.* Before delving into the above list of possibilities, we should consider why three are being proposed. Upon reviewing the available literature on this subject, it would appear that most of the critics of Grudem have favored arguments one and two, but have not offered the third view as a possibility. Grudem contradicts views one and two, while dismissing the third view with little effort. His critique is that without any *volition* on the part of the Jews to surrender Paul to the Romans, there is no sense in which one could say that Paul was *delivered over* (*paradōsousin* > *paradidōmi*):

> "The verb that Agabus used (*paradidōmi*, "to deliver, hand over") requires the sense of voluntarily, consciously, deliberately giving over or handing over something to someone else. That is the sense it has in all 119 other instances of the word in the New Testament. But that sense is not true with respect to the treatment of Paul by the Jews; they did not voluntarily hand Paul over to the Romans!"[107]

Grudem's most specific responses on this point have been directed to Robert L. Thomas and F. David Farnell.[108] Both Thomas and Farnell have written excellent works and yet they have not addressed, with requisite detail, many of Grudem's subsequent refutations on this subject. Because of this, I wish to point out to the reader the need for a more thorough response to Grudem's developed argument. The challenge of comprehending the volition of a mob may not at all be easy, especially since the Jewish assembly in Acts 21-23 wasn't entirely monolithic. It is interesting to note that by the time that we get to Acts 23 there are some in Jerusalem who sided with Paul, while others wanted to tear him "to pieces" (Acts 23:10). For that matter, those who conspired to take Paul

---

[107] Grudem, Systematic Theology, 1052.

[108] The three main critiques of Grudem mentioned in this book are: 1. Robert L. Thomas, "Prophecy Rediscovered? A Review of The Gift of Prophecy in the New Testament and Today," *Bibliotheca Sacra* (Dallas TX), Vol. 149 (1992): 82-96; 2. Thomas R. Edgar, Satisfied by the Promise of the Spirit, (Grand Rapids MI: Kregel Resources, 1996); and 3. F. David Farnell, Fallible New Testament Prophecy/Prophets? A Critique of Wayne Grudem's Hypothesis (Master's Seminary Journal).

from Roman custody in order to murder him themselves consisted of a small squadron of just over 40 men (Acts 23:12-22). The point is simply this: it is somewhat difficult to assume that any crowd or assembly would be monolithic in its motive and intent, at all times. This is only important when we attempt to consider the motive and intent of the Jews in view of Paul's capture in Jerusalem. With all of these issues in hand, we will more fully examine the three proposed views:

1. Paul was *delivered over* to his captors *despite the will of the Jewish mob*: This view does not focus on the mob's will or intent with respect to the Greek term, *paradidōmi*, but instead examines the crucial theme of Scripture dealing with God's sovereignty over the will and intent of man. The Scriptures clearly reveal that God uses the *direct* and *indirect* actions of men, as mediated by a wide range of human motives and intents.[109] Such examples of *direct and indirect human-agency* vary in their construct – but they always reveal the ultimate actions of God's sovereign volition, will, and providence among men. For example, Peter accuses the Jews of *volitionally delivering Christ over to be crucified* through the *instrumental actions* of the Gentiles, according to God's predetermined will... (Acts 2:23);[110] Paul attributes his God-given joy to the *instrumentality* of the *unwitting actions* of those who sought to do him harm while in prison (Phil 1:12-20); Joseph's blessings from God are attributed to the *instrumentality* of the *unwitting actions* of his brothers who, in jealousy, abandoned him as mere chattel (Gen 50:19-21); and

---

[109] Though the mob wanted Paul dead, the question about how such an end would be achieved was not at all monolithic. Once Roman intervention took place, the Jews' capacity to carry out their desired task had changed. Though their objective remained the same, the question of *means* had been modified. This is evident when we see that only a small band of "more than forty" Jews formed a plot to recapture Paul in order to murder him. To suggest that the Jews' had a monolithic sense about how they would rid themselves of the Apostle Paul simply misses too much of what is revealed in the narrative.

[110] This view is presented by Thomas and Farnell.

Israel is the *unintentional reconciler* of the Gentiles through their *volitional* rejection of the Messiah (John 11:47-53; Romans 11:15-22[111]). Though these constructs of attribution do vary, we see that in them all is the core lesson that it is God who works all things together for good, such that He *variously* utilizes the direct and indirect actions of men – whether those actions are done *intentionally, unintentionally, knowingly, or unknowingly*. It should be noted that Paul's particular teaching on this subject frequently provoked great hostility from the Jews, especially in relation to God's *sovereign will and volition* to bless the world with the Gospel *despite Israel's intent and volition*:

Romans 11:11 "...by their transgression salvation has come to the Gentiles, to make them jealous." (NASB95)

Though it is the case that the Jews exercised their own will and intent in the crucifixion of Christ, God was accomplishing His sovereign plan to have "salvation come to the Gentiles." In this we see an *asymmetry* between God's will (blessing the Gentiles) and the intent of the Jews

[111] The chief priests and Pharisees sought to murder Jesus so that the Romans would not come and take away both their "place" and "nation" (John 11:48). The Jews therefore accepted the words of Caiaphas that "it is expedient for you that one man die for the people, and that the whole nation not perish." Ironically, the Jews did not comprehend the fact that by these words God had revealed His authoritative "prophecy" through the mouth of Caiaphas, revealing God's ultimate design, as clarified by John: that "...Jesus was going to die for the nation, and not for the nation only, but in order that He might also gather together into one the children of God who are scattered abroad" (John 11:52). In God's sovereign Providence the nation of Israel became the instrument through which God brought reconciliation to the Gentiles (Romans 11:15). This He accomplished through the *instrumentality of the intentional, unintentional, witting, and unwitting actions of the Jews* who crucified Christ, for their self-preservation, through the *instrumentality of the Romans* who actually nailed Him to the cross (Acts 2:23). Once again, the ultimate lesson in all of this is that when it comes to the question of ultimate attribution, it is God who orchestrates all events in accordance with His divine plan for His ultimate glory (Romans 11:36).

(delivering Christ over to be crucified). Ironically, this Gospel truth of God's grace being extended to the Gentiles is one of the central reasons why the Jews sought Paul's execution:

> Acts 22:21–22 — 21 "And He said to me, 'Go! For I will send you far away to the Gentiles.' " 22 They listened to him up to this statement, and then they raised their voices and said, "Away with such a fellow from the earth, for he should not be allowed to live!"

As the Jews continued to resist Christ, the Gospel, and His messenger to the Gentiles, the blessings of the Gospel continued to spread to the world. In the end, Paul was delivered over to the Roman's by God's sovereign will *above any other will or intent.*

2. Paul *was delivered over* to his captors *by legal compulsion*: Similar to the previous view, this perspective is not focused on the will and intent of the Jewish mob with respect to the Greek term *paradidōmi*, but instead considers the compulsory nature of Paul's transition from Jewish to Roman authorities. Thus, this view sees the Jewish mob delivering Paul over to the Romans by bare compulsion. We have already discussed the compelling nature of Rome's anti-riot laws. Such laws made it so that anyone who instigated a riot could be liable for property damage, personal injury, or even be found guilty of treason, depending on the circumstances. Such historical background renders this certainty: *the act of instigating a riot could not be ignored by Roman authorities.* Of course, the real riot-makers were the Jews who "stirred up all the crowd" in Jerusalem (Acts 21:27); but only Paul was held as the suspicious party because of the continued complaints and accusations of the Jews. It is interesting to note that the Jews' true opposition to Paul had to do with theological issues relating to his teachings on Christ (Acts 18:5-6, 21:28a), the notion of salvation being extended to the Gentiles (Acts 22:21), and the presumption that he "desecrated the temple" with the presence of a

Gentile (Acts 21:28b). Yet, when Paul was in Caesarea, Tertullus presented his case before Felix with a very different focus:

> Acts 24:5–6: 5 "For we have found this man a real pest and a fellow who stirs up dissension among all the Jews throughout the world, and a ringleader of the sect of the Nazarenes. 6 "And he even tried to desecrate the temple; and then we arrested him. [We wanted to judge him according to our own Law...]"

The lack of emphasis on theology in Tertullus' complaint reveals the pragmatic and shifting tactics of the Jews. Paul's Roman captivity shifted the Jews' complaint against Paul, such that their chief concern about him was that he "stirs up dissension" among the Jewish people. Comprehending the gravity of being called a riot-maker, Paul responded with this defense:

> Acts 24:11–12: 11 since you can take note of the fact that no more than twelve days ago I went up to Jerusalem to worship. 12 "Neither in the temple, nor in the synagogues, nor in the city itself did they find me *carrying on a discussion with anyone or causing a riot.*" (Italics mine).

As long as Paul was blamed for inciting riotous behavior,[112] he would not be released without a proper and conclusive hearing. The Jews' violent opposition to Paul continued to secure his status as a prisoner of the

---

[112] Tertullus pressed this accusation against Paul in Acts 24:1–5 — 1 After five days the high priest Ananias came down with some elders, with an attorney named Tertullus, and they brought charges to the governor against Paul. 2 After Paul had been summoned, Tertullus began to accuse him, saying to the governor, "Since we have through you attained much peace, and since by your providence reforms are being carried out for this nation, 3 we acknowledge this in every way and everywhere, most excellent Felix, with all thankfulness. 4 "But, that I may not weary you any further, I beg you to grant us, by your kindness, a brief hearing. 5 "For we have found this man a real pest and a fellow who stirs up dissension among all the Jews throughout the world, and a ringleader of the sect of the Nazarenes.

Romans in Jerusalem, which began the chain of events that would eventually lead to his travels to Rome.[113]

> Acts 28:18–19: 18 "And when they had examined me, they were willing to release me because there was no ground for putting me to death. 19 "But when the Jews objected [*antilegontōn*], I was forced to appeal to Caesar, not that I had any accusation against my nation."

Even in this summary by Paul, it is clear that the unresolved opposition from the Jews further embedded Paul within Roman legal custody.[114] Unmistakably, from Jerusalem to Caesarea, the Jews' continual and public rejection of Paul necessitated these events, and, by God's sovereign direction of human agency, everything was happening right on time. These observations help us to understand the manner in which the Jewish mob sought Paul's death beneath the pressing reality of Roman law. It also reveals the changing dynamic of their cooperation with, and

---

[113] Interestingly, even for those who wish to stress *volitional symmetry* between the intent of the Jews and the Romans' actions, we should note that the Jews' ultimate goal of murdering Paul was fulfilled by the hands of the Romans in the end. Their shouts of rejection - "away with this fellow from the earth, for he should not be allowed to live" were fully realized when the Apostle was beheaded by the instrumentality of Roman authority. It is commonly held that Paul was executed while in Rome (mid 60s AD) under the rule of Nero. John Fox records the account as follows: "Paul, the apostle, who before was called Saul, after his great travail and unspeakable labors in promoting the Gospel of Christ, suffered also in this first persecution under Nero. Abdias, declareth that under his execution Nero sent two of his esquires, Ferega and Parthemius, to bring him word of his death." If this is the case, then the cry of the Jews was fulfilled by such martyrdom: "Away with such a fellow from the earth, for he should not be allowed to live!" John Fox, <u>Fox's Book of Martyrs</u>, ed., William Byron Forbush, D.D., (Philadelphia: The John C. Winston Company), 4.

[114] *"I was forced to appeal"* [*ēnagkasthēn*]. When translating a single verb into English, it is necessary to supply what are called *notional* and *auxiliary* verbs. The notional verb in question is *"appeal,"* while the auxiliary verbs are *"was forced."* The auxiliary verbs are necessary in order to convey, correctly, the notion of passivity since *ēnagkasthēn* is an aorist *passive* indicative verb. Paul was the one making the appeal, but it was the Jewish mob who *compelled* that action.

submission to, their Roman overlords. This leads us to our third and final view: Paul was *willingly delivered over* by the Jews in the face of Roman jurisprudence:

3. Paul was *willingly delivered over* by the Jews in the face of *Roman jurisprudence*: As previously mentioned, this particular view has been rendered as an impossibility by Grudem since, as he argues, "the verb that Agabus used (*paradidōmi*, "to deliver, hand over") requires the sense of voluntarily, consciously, deliberately giving over or handing over something to someone else."[115] In this section, we will accept Grudem's supposition concerning the word *paradidōmi*, even though there are still outstanding questions that remain regarding such a monolithic connotation of the term.[116] In this section, we will examine Grudem's assertion that the Jewish crowd never delivered Paul over to their Roman overlords *volitionally*. To do this we will consider three important, interpretive factors within this section: a. Paul's own testimony concerning these events; b. The interactions between the Romans and the Jewish mob; and c. A comparison between Paul's and Christ's arrest.

3.a. Paul's Own Testimony Concerning These Events: When Paul was in Rome, he gave testimony concerning his transference from Jewish legal

---

[115] Grudem, Systematic Theology, 1052.

[116] "*paradidōmi* describes an act where the subject (one party) has custody or possession of someone or something and hands it over into the custody of another party. It has nothing to do with the attitude of the subject involved. Attitude can only be determined from the context or in some few cases where the verb itself implies the attitude such as to rejoice or to be sorry. For an illustration, a soldier returning from a holiday may say 'I am reporting for duty.' The subject does the action, but this does not mean the soldier would come in voluntarily if he did not need to...nor does this change the meaning of the expression 'reporting for duty' to happily or enthusiastically reporting for duty. Also, 'volunteering to enlist' means to enlist on one's own. It is not concerned with other pressures, or how willingly the person enlisted." Thomas R. Edgar, September 30th 2013, "*Paradidōmi* Response," personal e-mail.

authorities to the Romans indicating that he was "delivered [*paradothēn*][117] as a prisoner from Jerusalem into the hands of the Romans":

> Acts 28:17–19: 17 After three days Paul called together those who were the leading men of the Jews, and when they came together, he began saying to them, "Brethren, though I had done nothing against our people or the customs of our fathers, yet I was delivered [*paradothēn*] as a prisoner from Jerusalem into the hands of the Romans. 18 "And when they had examined me, they were willing to release me because there was no ground for putting me to death. 19 "But when the Jews objected, I was forced to appeal to Caesar, not that I had any accusation against my nation."

Grudem's response to these passages is as follows:

> "The Greek text of Acts 28:17 explicitly refers to Paul's transfer *out of* Jerusalem as *a prisoner*.[118] Therefore Paul's statement describes his transfer out of the Jewish judicial system (the Jews were seeking to bring him again to be examined by the Sanhedrin in Acts 23:15, 20) and into the Roman judicial system at Caesarea (Acts 23:23-35). Therefore Paul correctly says in Acts 28:18 that the same Romans into whose hands he had been delivered as a prisoner (v. 17) were the ones who (Gk. *oitines*, v. 18), 'When they had examined me...wished to set me at liberty, because there was no reason for the death penalty in my case" (Acts 28:18; cf. 23:29; also 25:11, 18-19; 26:31-32). Then Paul adds that when the Jews objected he was compelled 'to appeal to Caesar' (Acts 28:19; cf. 25:11). This whole narrative in Acts 28:17-19 refers to Paul's

---

[117] G. *paradothen* 1ps aorist passive indicative. Agabus used word in This is what the Holy Spirit says: 'In this way the Jews at Jerusalem will bind the man who owns this belt and *deliver* [*paradōsousin* 3pp future active indicative] him into the hands of the Gentiles.'

[118] Grudem's note at this point is as follows: "The NIV translation, 'I was arrested *in* Jerusalem and handed over to the Romans,' completely misses the idea (which the Greek text requires) of being delivered *out of* (*ex*) Jerusalem, and removes the idea that he was delivered as a prisoner (Gk. *desmois*), adding rather the idea that he was arrested in Jerusalem, an event that is not metioned [*sic*] in the Greek text of this verse." Grudem, Systematic Theology, 1052.

transfer out of Jerusalem to Caesarea in Acts 23:12-35, and explains to the Jews in Rome why Paul is in Roman custody."[119]

I believe that Grudem is correct to understand Paul's expression, *"I was delivered as a prisoner from Jerusalem into the hands of the Romans,"* as referring to his transference from *one legal authority to another, i.e. the Jewish judicial system to the Roman judicial system.* However, Grudem's *application* of this thought is corrupted through a misunderstanding of some important historical facts. Paul was actually removed from *all Jewish legal authority* the moment he was originally arrested by the Romans in Acts 21:33. Though Paul was briefly released from his bonds in Acts 22:40, in order to testify to the Jews a second time (Acts 23:1-6), he remained under Roman authority and supervision throughout his stay in Jerusalem. In fact, when the conspirators in Acts 23:12-15 sought to bring Paul to a *faux* trial before the Sanhedrin, in order to murder him by stealth, they knew that they would have to appeal to the Roman commander for Paul's release. This demonstrates Paul's uninterrupted Roman custody while he was in Jerusalem.[120] After Paul's Roman arrest in Acts 21, the Sanhedrin had no authority over Paul whatsoever. Thus, the actual point of legal transition came in Acts 21:33 when he was placed *in Roman hands under Roman rule.* Grudem denies that there is any connection between Acts 28:17 and Paul's arrest by the Romans while in Jerusalem. He does this, in part, by arguing that *paradidōmi* indicates that the Jews had no intention to surrender Paul to their Roman

---

[119] Ibid.

[120] The son of Paul's sister, who became aware of this plot, was brought to the commander and informed him as follows: Acts 23:18–20: 18 So he took him and led him to the commander and said, *"Paul the prisoner* called me to him and asked me to lead this young man to you since he has something to tell you." 19 The commander took him by the hand and stepping aside, began to inquire of him privately, "What is it that you have to report to me?" 20 And he said, "The Jews *have agreed to ask you* to bring Paul down tomorrow to the Council, as though they were going to inquire somewhat more thoroughly about him" (italics mine).

overlords. Yet Grudem's argument is relegated to a limited analysis of Acts 21, while failing to address the contiguous reality of Paul's *arrest*, *testimony*, and *interaction* with his accusers in Acts 21:33-23:22. This is unfortunate, because it overlooks important details regarding Paul's legal status throughout his stay in Jerusalem, and it also ignores important facts about Roman laws and customs. Paul could have been released back to his Jewish captors, but for this to happen he would have to be given an opportunity to make a *complete and uninterrupted defense* before his accusers, as Festus reminded King Agrippa:

> Acts 25:16: "... it is not the custom of the Romans to hand over any man before the accused meets his accusers face to face and has an opportunity to make his defense against the charges."

Roman law strongly protected the rights of the accused,[121] a reality that afforded Paul continued protection from Jerusalem to Rome. Lysias gave Paul such an opportunity of self-defense when he *granted him permission to speak* to the Jewish assembly (Acts 21:40-22:1-21), but Paul was interrupted before he could complete his testimony (Acts 22:22). From this point on, Paul was never again placed under Jewish legal authority. In view of all these details, Grudem is simply wrong when he links Acts 28:17 to Paul's transfer to Caesarea. Grudem's avoidance of the full context of Acts 21:40-23:22 and misuse of Acts 28:17-19 is simply striking. As well, his insistence that the Jews never possessed any *volition* in the matter of delivering Paul over to their legal overlords is unpersuasive, as we shall see in the following:

3.b. The Interactions Between the Romans and the Jewish Mob: Luke supplies very interesting details concerning how the Jewish mob interacted with their Roman overlords as Paul was *arrested, testified,* and

---

[121] Andrew Borkowski LLB, <u>Textbook on Roman Law</u>, (NY: New York, Oxford University Press, 1997), 70.

interacted with his accusers. The three aforementioned Roman seizures (in which Paul was removed from the presence of the Jews) are very important and will be expanded below:

3.b.1. Acts 21:33-34: Paul was arrested by the Roman commander and was ordered to be taken from the midst of the Jewish mob and "brought"[122] into the barracks. The verb used by Luke (brought > *agesthai*) denotes a simple action of removal, which is strikingly different from the commander's act of taking Paul away from the mob "by force" [*arpasai*] in Acts 23:10.[123] Prior to the order in Acts 21:34, the commander was able to speak to the crowd such that he attempted to ascertain "who he [Paul] was and what he had done." However, once the commander gave the order to have Paul brought back to the barracks, the crowd's initial complicity gave way to violence such that Paul had to be carried away (*bastazesthai* – Acts 21:35). In this first incident alone, we see the manner in which the mob was able to shift from civility to violence in very little time.

3.b.2. Acts 21:40-22:24: Having failed to ascertain a clear charge from Paul's accusers, the commander gave Paul permission to testify before the Jews (Acts 21:40a); Luke says that "there was a great hush" that overcame the previously outspoken mob (Acts 21:40b), revealing the Jews' understanding of the seriousness of the legal proceeding that was about to take place; Paul then

---

[122] "...he ordered him to be brought (*agesthai*) into the barracks" because of the "uproar" (*thorubon*) of the mob. The verb *agesthai* (from G. *agō*) is a general term used to speak of the movement or transference of someone or something. It in no way carries the force of thought of what followed when Paul had to be carried (*bastazesthai*) because of the violence of the mob.

[123] Edgar argues that the Jews' volitional act of delivering Paul over to the Romans is evident in Acts 21:34 by virtue of Luke's contrasting choice of the verb *arpasai* in Acts 23:10 (*arpasai*: aorist active infinitive of *arpazō*): "Later (Acts 23:10) the centurion specifically commands his soldiers to take Paul from the council 'by force,' using a different verb, *arpazō*. This implies that this was not the case in the first event. In Acts 21, the Jews handed Paul over." Edgar, "*Paradidōmi* Response."

delivered his lengthiest defense (Acts 22:1-21).[124] Within his testimony, Paul spoke of Christ, his own conversion, and his calling to be a witness to the Gentiles. Paul's mention of God's grace being extended to the Gentiles proved to be too much for his audience, therefore, this formerly "hushed" assembly erupted with their response: *"Away with such a fellow from the earth [aire apo tēs gēs]*, for he should not be allowed to live!" (Acts 22:22). All of this took place while Paul was being directed through the normal legal proceedings due to any Roman prisoner. The appeal that Paul *"should not be allowed to live,"* was similarly delivered to Festus when the Jews, once again, cried out for Paul's execution: "...the Jews appealed to me, both at Jerusalem and here, *loudly declaring that he ought not to live any longer*. But I found that he had committed nothing worthy of death..." (Festus, in Acts 25:24–25, italics mine). The Jews' cry to Festus (*"he ought not to live any longer"*) and to the commander (*"he should not be allowed to live!"* Acts 22:22) reveals an unmistakable *appeal [enetuchon]* for Paul's death by Roman hands. In Acts 22, as the Jewish mob cried for Paul's death, the commander ordered Paul to be "brought" *[eisagesthai]* into the barracks (Acts 22:24). Luke's use of the word *eisagesthai* points to a simple transfer of Paul by the Romans.[125] This same term, *eisagesthai*, is also used in Acts 21:29 referring to the Jews' presumption that Paul took Trophimus and *brought him into [eisēgagen]* the temple. As in Acts 22:24, the term denotes a *peaceful action* rather than a *forceful one*. In contrast to Acts 21:35 and Acts 23:10, this suggests *maximal cooperation* from the mob. Clearly, the commander brought Paul to the barracks, not for his protection, but so that he would be scourged and questioned as "they stretched him out with thongs." At this point in the narrative, Paul's greatest danger was not the Jewish mob, but the Romans who began to torture him; that is, until they discovered that Paul was a Roman citizen (Acts 22:25-29).

---

[124] "Brethren and fathers, hear my defense [*apologias*] which I now offer to you." Acts 22:1. Paul also testified to the Jews in Acts 23:1-6, after he was released from his bonds by Lysias, but he didn't get very far at all and the divided mob degraded into confusion.

[125] In Acts 21:35, Paul had to be carried away because of the violence of the mob, and in Acts 23:10 he was taken "by force" [*arpasai*]. However, in Acts 22:24 Paul was simply *brought to [eisagesthai]* the barracks.

3.b.3. Acts 22:30-23:10: The commander's attempt for a retrial on Paul's behalf would have been a highly provocative act in the eyes of the Jews. They already made their appeal for Paul's death, but this did not end matters. Remaining under Roman authority, Paul was released from his bonds in order to appear before the Sanhedrin and answer to his accusers a second time. It is important to note that Paul remained under Roman authority, though to some in the crowd it may have appeared otherwise due to the absence of his bonds.[126] Luke reminds us of Paul's legal standing when he indicates that the commander *ordered* the Council to assemble, he *brought* Paul, and *set* him before them:

> Acts 22:30: But on the next day, wishing to know for certain why he had been accused by the Jews, *he released* him and *ordered* the chief priests and all the Council to assemble, and *brought* Paul down and *set* him before them. (italics mine).

Under the commander's directive, Paul made his second attempted defense before his accusers, but it was short lived when the Jewish mob responded with confusion. Some supported Paul while others resisted with an abundance of violence such that the commander *seized Paul by force* (*arpasai*) from the reach of the mob[127] for fear that he would be torn to pieces (Acts 23:10).[128] This term, *arpasai*, speaks of a similar forcefulness to that which was applied when Paul was carried away from the violent mob after his arrest (Acts 21:35). Unlike the unified state of the mob, as evidenced by their clear appeal in Acts 22:22, the Jews became splintered and divided once it became clear that Paul had a number of defenders among some of the Pharisees and the Romans.

---

[126] It may be that the absence of Paul's bonds gave the appearance, to some, that Paul spoke to the Jews as a free man. If some perceived this, they would have assumed that Paul was once again accessible for their murderous plot.

[127] Acts 23:18-20.

[128] It is interesting that the defenders of Paul who said, "We find nothing wrong with this man," were the ones who argued *heatedly* [*diemaxonto* – to strongly protest, *Acts 23:10*] in defense of the apostle. Thus, the nature of the crowd's hostility, along with the commander's fears, remains somewhat uncertain. Yet, one thing that is certain is that the mob no longer spoke with one voice as it had in Acts 22:22.

When we compare these incidents, it becomes quite clear that the mob's reactions to Roman authorities changed considerably in each case. This is important when we consider the question of the mob's intention, especially regarding a willful delivery of Paul over to the Romans. The commander's attempt to carry out his threefold duty of *1. Arresting Paul; 2. Giving him an opportunity to testify before his accusers; and 3. Allowing his accusers an opportunity to respond* was all quite challenging. He attempted to ascertain their charges three times (Acts 21:33, 40; 22:30). His first and third attempt to ascertain Paul's guilt was met with confusion. However, his second attempt to discern the will of the mob (Acts 21:40-22:22) resulted in a clear and unified cry for Paul's execution. Recognizing the realities of Roman authority amidst Paul's legal proceedings, the Jews responded quite clearly within this narrative. Here and only here do we find the mob speaking as with one voice:

In Jerusalem: Paul is "Bound" and "Delivered Over"			
#	Text	Paul	Romans/Commander	Jewish Mob
1	Acts 21:30-31	Arrested by Jews	Not yet on scene	Seeks to kill him
2	Acts 21:32-33	1st Seizure & arrest by Romans	Questions Jews & takes Paul away	Paul's defense to Jews not yet given
3	Acts 21:40-22:22	Paul testifies and is "delivered over..." via the Jewish mob	Afforded Paul his legal right to address his accusers	"away with him...he does not deserve to live!"
4	Acts 22:23-29	2nd Seizure by Romans	Paul – still a prisoner: examined, scourged...	Not present in Antonia Fortress
5	Acts 23:1-9	Paul testifies to the Council under Roman authority	Paul – still a prisoner brought before the Council without bonds	Crowd is confused - Some side with Paul, others seek to kill him
6	Acts 23:10	3rd Seizure by Romans	Fearful that "Paul would be torn to pieces"	Plot by some to assassinate Paul

In light of these contextual considerations, along with the mob's unified cry, *"away with such a fellow from the earth, for he should not be allowed to live!"* we see that the Apostle Paul faced remarkable rejection from his

Jewish kinsmen in a manner highly reflective of Christ's own suffering and rejection.

3.c. The Parallel Between Christ and Paul: We often think of Christ's trial and execution in far more simplified terms, and yet the Savior's pathway to the cross was paved with some rather striking legal gymnastics. We should remember that earlier in Christ's ministry, the Jews wanted to kill Him *directly* on several occasions. Yet, the plan to have Him murdered through the instrumentality of Roman authority did not come until much later. In the end, the Jews came to terms with the complexities and problems associated with killing Jesus directly in view of Roman law:

> John 18:31: So Pilate said to them, "Take Him yourselves, and judge Him according to your law." The Jews said to him, "We are not permitted to put anyone to death..."

As we follow the plot to have Christ murdered by the Romans, we see a strong trail of pragmatism and deceit along the way. Before Roman involvement, the Jews accused Christ of being in violation of Jewish laws and customs. These charges were maintained until Christ was ushered into the Roman courts. Then and only then do we find the Jewish leaders feigning concern about paying taxes and honoring Caesar. The fact that he was charged with inciting rebellion (Luke 23:14) brings us once again to the grave reality Rome's anti-riot laws. Luke and John's parallel accounts give us such a picture:

> Luke 23:14: ...and [Pilate] said to them, "You brought this man to me as one who incites the people to rebellion, and behold, having examined Him before you, I have found no guilt in this man regarding the charges which you make against Him."

John 19:12–15: 12 As a result of this Pilate made efforts to release Him, but the Jews cried out saying, "If you release this Man, you are no friend of Caesar; everyone who makes himself out to be a king opposes Caesar." 13 Therefore when Pilate heard these words, he brought Jesus out, and sat down on the judgment seat at a place called The Pavement, but in Hebrew, Gabbatha. 14 Now it was the day of preparation for the Passover; it was about the sixth hour. And he said to the Jews, "Behold, your King!" 15 So they cried out, "Away with Him, away with Him, crucify Him!" Pilate said to them, "Shall I crucify your King?" The chief priests answered, "We have no king but Caesar."

During the trial, the Jews sought any charge that would lead to Christ's death. So desperate were they to see Christ murdered, that they regurgitated this blasphemy: *"if you release this Man, you are no friend of Caesar...we have no king but Caesar."* The irony of this final moment is difficult to express, yet we find that the presence of Roman authority affected the masses remarkably, resulting in several disingenuous appeals and accusations. During the trial, when Pilate offered the choice between Christ and Barabbas, the mob required some significant persuasion in order to make the "right" choice:

Matthew 27:20: But the chief priests and the elders persuaded the crowds to ask for Barabbas and to put Jesus to death.

Clearly, this was not a principled mob. The religious leaders shifted in their accusations against Christ, moving from theological concerns to complaints against Christ's disloyalty to Caesar. Neither was the mob monolithic in its thinking throughout the trial, from beginning to end. Their choices and actions changed considerably throughout the legal proceedings of Christ's trial. In all of this, I would suggest to the reader that this provides a crucial parallel to Paul's own interaction with the Jews and the Romans, especially when we try to think about what the Jewish mob *intended* with respect to Paul. In the case of Christ, three key phases of his trial reveal the core requirements of Roman law: *Christ was placed under Roman arrest; He was given the opportunity to respond to His accusers; and his accusers gave their response, demanding His death in the presence of Roman authorities.* Beneath such authority, there would be no sense in which Christ could be killed by any other means. It is this pressing reality of Roman legal authority that is very significant, such that even the Jews admitted that they were *not permitted to put Christ to death.* The fear of Roman retribution made the prospect of capital punishment, by Jewish authorities, very dangerous. The desperation of the Jews to have Christ murdered was so great that they degraded from their true, more ideological charges against the Savior, to the contrived charges of *tax evasion, creating riots, and instigating rebellion against Caesar.* Thus, while shackled as a Roman prisoner, Christ heard the mob cry out at His public hearing: *"Away with Him, away with Him, crucify Him!" [aron aron, staurōson auton – "Away, away, crucify Him"].*[129] With the fullness of this cry, it was evident that the Jewish mob desired that Christ would be removed *by means of death on a cross by the hands of their Roman overlords.* Moreover, this wish of theirs was granted by Pilate who, humanly speaking, possessed *sole authority* over Christ's life or death; which brings us once again to that important moment when Paul heard similar words from his kinsmen according to the flesh:

> Acts 22:21–22: 21 "And He said to me, 'Go! For I will send you far away to the Gentiles.' " 22 They listened to him up to this statement, and then they raised their voices and said, "Away with such a fellow from the earth, for he should not be allowed to live!"

As already mentioned, the appeal that Paul *"should not be allowed to live"* was similarly delivered to Festus when the Jews, again, cried out for Paul's execution (*"he ought not to live any longer"* Acts 25:24). This "appeal" [*entuchon*] to the authority of Festus shows that the Jews understood their legal posture before the Roman authorities. By this parallel, we see

---

[129] John 19:15.

that the intent of the mob's cry in Acts 22:22 was quite clear, and their expression, "*Away* with such a fellow *from the earth*," would have been hauntingly familiar as it reflected the stark language used to speak of the Messiah's anticipated death:

Isaiah 53:8: "...For his life is taken *away from the earth* [*airetai apo tēs gēs*]: because of the iniquities of my people he was led to death." [LXX, italics mine]

Similar to Christ, *Paul was placed under Roman arrest; he was given the opportunity to respond to his accusers; and in response, the mob demanded his death in the presence of Roman authorities. Beneath such authority, there would be no sense in which he could be killed by any other means.* Acts 22:21-22 offers an important perspective on Paul's arrest because it reveals a key step in Rome's legal process. This moment is also important seeing that it reveals the harmonious desire of the mob. However, had the Jews listened to Paul's testimony, he could have been released for their own purposes; but as it is, they interrupted him, demanding his death, and thus securing his Roman custody even further (Acts 25:16).

It is important to remember that, from the standpoint of Roman law, Paul's *arrest, initial testimony, and response from his accusers* was a single, legal event (Acts 21:33-22:22), all of which revealed the Jews' act of delivering Paul over to their Roman overlords *willingly, in submission to Roman jurisprudence.* This weighty reality of Roman legal authority is significant. It should remind us that when the Jews cried out, *"Away with such a fellow from the earth, for he should not be allowed to live!" (Acts 22:22)* they did so in the presence of those who held *sole authority* over Paul's life or death. Moreover, this same plea for Paul's death followed him *while he remained in the hands of the Romans*:

Acts 23:29: 29 and I found him to be accused over questions about their Law, *but under no accusation deserving death or imprisonment.*

Acts 25:11: 11 *"If, then, I am a wrongdoer and have committed anything worthy of death*, I do not refuse to die; but if none of those things is true of which these men accuse me, no one can hand me over to them. I appeal to Caesar."

With a cursory reading of Acts 21:15-23:30, we may miss the profundity of the Jews' cry for Paul's death in Acts 22:22. In order to presume that the Jews were not willing to have the Romans kill Paul, we would have to assume the following:

- In order to accept *fallible prophecy's* interpretation of Agabus we would have to believe that there are no significant parallels between the Jews' rejection of Paul and Christ. For this we would have to ignore the parallel contexts of the Jews' appeal to the Roman authorities for the death of Christ ("Away with *Him*, away with *Him*, crucify Him!" John 19:15) as well as the Jews' appeal to the Roman authorities for the death of Paul ("Away with such a fellow from the earth, for he should not be allowed to live!" Acts 22:22).

- Along with this, we would have to reject or ignore the Scriptural parallels between Acts 22:22 and Acts 25:24-25, thus nullifying the corroborating testimony of Festus who understood the Jews' cry for Paul's death as an appeal (*enetuchon*) for action by Roman authorities.

- In view of this, acceptance of *fallible prophecy* leads us to alternate interpretations of the Jews' appeal for Paul's death in Acts 22:22. Thus, their unified cry, *"away with such a fellow from the earth, for he should not be allowed to live,"* would have to be interpreted as *a demand by the Jews to kill Paul, a Roman prisoner, themselves.* This would be nothing less than a provocative act of defiance against Roman law and authority (John 18:31) contradicting the relative ease with which Paul was ushered away [*eisagesthai*] from the crowd (Acts 22:24). This would also constitute a tactical contradiction to the stealth applied in the assassination plot hatched by some in Acts 23:12-15. Not only did they not have authority to kill citizens in general, but they most certainly had no license to seize and kill a Roman prisoner who was fiercely guarded by the requirements of Roman law. It is simply unthinkable that the Jews would publicize their plans to commit *the unlawful murder of a Roman prisoner* in the presence of the Roman commander and his soldiers. In such a case as this, we would have to believe that such open resistance to Roman authority was made in complete disregard for Rome's strict anti-riot laws. Thus, such an *outcry of rebellion, we would have to believe,* took place on the steps of the Roman barracks (Antonia Fortress), fully arrayed with the commander and his armed soldiers. Such a unified and open defiance like this would have made them all guilty of a riotous rebellion, as in the case of the Egyptian who "stirred up a revolt and led the four thousand men of the Assassins out into the wilderness."[130]

- On the other hand, ignoring the aforementioned options, an alternate position would be to believe that the Jews had no serious consideration of Rome's authority over Paul's life and death, and therefore they had no thought or hope that he could be convicted and executed by the Romans, despite the historical reality of Christ's own trial and crucifixion. Thus, their outcry would then be interpreted as nothing more than an ineffectual wish. Yet, such an assumption contradicts the force of their *cry:* "*away [aire]*[131] with such a fellow from the earth, for he should not be allowed to live!"

Moreover, we should wonder why the Jews did not demand Paul's release so that they could murder him in secret. Such an idea became central to the "more than forty" who conspired to kill Paul in stealth. To assume that the Jews did not intend, in the unique moment of Acts 22:22, to have their Roman overlords carry out the task of killing Paul requires a strong measure of imagination; after all, a Roman execution would have been so much easier. Why would they risk so much by interrupting Paul's defense *if they did not intend for the Roman commander to carry out their deed for them*? Are we to assume that their appeal for Paul's death was a demand

---

[130] Acts 21:38.

[131] Acts 22:22: G. *aire* – 2PS present active imperative of *airō*.

that they do it themselves, in open and public defiance of Roman law?[132] If this is the case, then why was Paul escorted [*eisagesthai*] from this scene with such ease? Such thinking simply does not comport with the facts at hand. A more normal reading of this entire section would lead us to see the shifting pragmatism of the Jews. They wanted Paul dead, but if this meant the Romans carrying out the deed, as in the case of Christ, then so be it – *he should not be allowed to live.* Though some still plotted to assassinate Paul in stealth, the broader Jewish assembly later appealed to the one who held Paul's life in his hands - Festus, the Roman procurator of Judea (Acts 25:24). Despite these consistent appeals for Paul's death, the Roman authorities from Jerusalem to Caesarea never found a basis for his death. When Lysias momentarily released Paul from his bonds (Acts 22:30), allowing him to speak to his accusers once again, the Jews reacted with an abundance of resistance. These early signs of Lysias' willingness to release Paul led some of the Jews to seek out the covert tactics of assassination (Acts 23:12-22). Lysias forwarded his findings of Paul's innocence to Felix, and as the Roman authorities continued to demonstrate a willingness to release Paul (Acts 24-26), the Jews continued to pursue him, appealing to the Roman authorities for his death, all of which led to Paul's appeal to Caesar in Rome.[133] In all of this, I would

---

[132] The case of the Jerusalem riot had not yet been settled. This fact is made apparent when Paul testified before Felix in Caesarea, "Neither in the temple, nor in the synagogues, nor in the city itself did they find me carrying on a discussion with anyone or causing a riot...but there were some Jews from Asia – who ought to have been present before you and to make accusation, if they should have anything against me" (Acts 24:12, 17-19). The true source of the uproar of the crowd came not from Paul, but from these Jews from Asia: "When the seven days were almost over, the Jews from Asia, upon seeing him in the temple, began to stir up all the crowd and laid hands on him..." (Acts 21:27).

[133] The willingness of the Romans to release Paul started in Jerusalem, with Lysias, and continued on to Paul's hearings in Caesarea: Acts 23:29 [Lysias]: "and I found him to be accused over questions about their Law, but under no accusation deserving death or imprisonment."; Acts 25:24–25 [Festus and Agrippa]: 24 Festus said, "King Agrippa, and all you gentlemen here present with us, you see this man about whom all the people of the Jews appealed to me, both at Jerusalem and here, loudly declaring that he ought not to live

submit to the reader that Paul's summary of events in Acts 28:17-19 comports clearly and perfectly with what we read in Acts 21:15-23:30, such that Paul was delivered over to the hands of the Romans *just as Agabus prophesied*:

> "The assertion that Paul was not handed over to the Gentiles as Agabus said is a statement that contradicts Paul himself. Describing the events to the elders in Rome, Paul said about himself, 'yet was I delivered prisoner from Jerusalem into the hands of the Romans" (Acts 28:17). Here he uses exactly the same verb as Agabus to describe this event (*paradidōmi*, 'deliver'). Paul describes this event in the same way as Agabus, and Paul, more than anyone else, should know what happened and be able to state it correctly and accurately."[134]

Of the three proposed viewpoints above, I would suggest that the narrative of Acts 21:15-23:30 reveals a strong harmony between them, with God's sovereignty reigning supremely overall. When we recognize that the Jews were overwhelmed by the force of Roman legal authority (Acts 21:33), it becomes evident that they eventually surrendered to such authority with the hope that Paul would be eliminated by their Roman overlords (Acts 22:22). Paul's *arrest, public testimony*, along with the *response from the mob* constitutes a composite legal event by which Paul was delivered over *willingly* by the Jews to the Roman authorities. In all of this, we see the harmony of God's providence in delivering Paul over so that Christ's chosen instrument would bear the Savior's name "before the Gentiles and kings and the sons of Israel" (Acts 9:15-16). However, if we were to remain in Acts 21 in our analysis of things, we would never see

---

any longer. 25 "But I found that he had committed nothing worthy of death; and since he himself appealed to the Emperor, I decided to send him." and Acts 26:30–32: 30 The king stood up and the governor and Bernice, and those who were sitting with them, 31 and when they had gone aside, they began talking to one another, saying, "This man is not doing anything worthy of death or imprisonment." 32 And Agrippa said to Festus, "This man might have been set free if he had not appealed to Caesar."
[134] Edgar, Satisfied by the Promise of the Holy Spirit, 82.

such a majestic view of God's providence; nor would we see the glory of the Holy Spirit who revealed these matters through Agabus; nor would we see the dignity of His prophet who ministered as a *true* prophet *by the Spirit*. It is quite stunning that Grudem limits himself when evaluating the question of fulfillment within the narrative of Acts. If we are going to accuse a prophet of error, then much more exegetical diligence must be applied. Thus, any attempt to discern the fulfillment of Agabus' prophecy with nothing more than Acts 21:31-35 is simply inadequate.

Some Practical Implications of Fallible Prophecy

We now come to the important matter of considering some of the implications of fallible prophecy. If *fallible prophecy* is to be considered as valid, then what kind of ministry practices should we expect to see in the local church? If Agabus' example were to be applied, by the interpretive standards of *fallible prophecy*, then where would this leave us?

It would leave us in very murky and dangerous territory.

Much of this murkiness comes from the confusion that is inherent in the judgment against Agabus: that he prophesied in error. When we consider the manner in which Grudem parses Agabus' prophecy, such inherent confusion becomes quite evident:

"Now it might be argued that Luke has no intention of showing that Agabus gave an inaccurate prophecy. These are really only differences in detail, someone might say. However, this explanation does not take full enough account of the fact that these are the only two details Agabus mentions-they are, in terms of content, the heart of his prophecy. In fact, these details are what make it unusual as a prediction. Probably anyone who knew how the Jews throughout the Empire had treated Paul in various cities could have 'predicted' with no revelation from the Holy Spirit at all that Paul would meet violent opposition from the Jews in Jerusalem. What was unique about Agabus's prophecy was this prediction of 'binding' and 'delivering into the hands of the Gentiles.' And on these two key elements, he is just a bit wrong."[135]

Grudem seems to have difficulty with his own prescription of sorting through what is most central to a

The "Fallible" Prophecy of Agabus	
"This is what the Holy Spirit says: 'In this way the Jews at Jerusalem will bind* the man who owns this belt and deliver* him into the hands of the Gentiles.' "	
TRUE Arrest in Jerusalem	"FALSE": Bound by Jews... "FALSE": Delivered over...

given prophecy. In the above text he says that "the only two details [*binding and delivering*] Agabus mentions-they are, in terms of content, the heart of his prophecy." Elsewhere, he refers to Agabus' two "errors" as being "minor" and that "he would have the general idea correct (Paul would be imprisoned at Jerusalem), but the details somewhat wrong."[136] This raises questions about how one should sort out what is the "heart" of any prophecy. If the responsibility of the advocates of *fallible prophecy* is to harvest out and retain *the heart* of any prophecy, then we might wonder how this would apply to Agabus himself, especially if the heart of his prophecy did not consist of the *truth of Paul's arrest*, but rather the *means by which he was arrested.* It should be noted at this point that the interpretation which sees Agabus' prophecy as being true renders an abundance of clarity; however, the interpretation which sees Agabus as uttering error renders confusion and more questions than answers. Moreover, even if we could accept the premise of *fallible prophecy,* then we would have to believe that, in all of Holy Writ, the New Testament church has been left with a miniscule example of such a "gift" in the case of Agabus. As well, when it comes to the *practical question of a believer's proper interaction with fallible prophecy,* Agabus' example supplies a troubling precedent. Consider what follows after Agabus' prophecy:

---

[135] Grudem, The Gift of Prophecy, 79.
[136] Ibid., 80.

Acts 21:11–13: 11 And coming to us, he took Paul's belt and bound his own feet and hands, and said, "This is what the Holy Spirit says: 'In this way the Jews at Jerusalem will bind the man who owns this belt and deliver him into the hands of the Gentiles.' " 12 When we had heard this, we as well as the local residents began begging him not to go up to Jerusalem. 13 Then Paul answered, "What are you doing, weeping and breaking my heart? For I am ready not only to be bound, but even to die at Jerusalem for the name of the Lord Jesus."

Luke and the local residents begged Paul not to go up to Jerusalem. According to the advocates of *fallible prophecy*, such resistance is attributable to the reality and presence of error in Agabus' utterance. As Grudem has said:

> Luke's "...larger purpose in the section...is no doubt to show the contrast between Paul's sure knowledge of God's will...and the uncertain grasp of God's will possessed by the prophets and other disciples whom Paul meets (Acts 21:4, 12-14) and who try to dissuade him from going to Jerusalem."[137]

One of the main premises of *fallible prophecy* is that such prophecies can rightfully be resisted since they contain a blend of truth and error. The overarching question amidst such a proposed ministry and practice is this: *How can one know what is to be resisted and what should be accepted?* The typical approach of *fallible prophecy* is to sift through and tease out error if a prophecy is theological in nature. However, when exhortative or predictive utterances are offered, then scriptural objectivity is supplanted by a universe of human subjectivity. According to Grudem, Luke and the local residents of Caesarea opposed Agabus' prophecy due to the "uncertain grasp of God's will" possessed by Agabus and the others. This is counted as a part of the "sifting" process that is considered to be a good and acceptable consequence of God's "gift" of *fallible prophecy* to the church. Moreover, edification is said to be the result of such *fallible*

---

[137] Ibid., 81.

prophecy, the importance of which is so great that believers are enjoined to *desire earnestly such a "gift" (1 Corinthians 14:1).* When we consider all such thoughts together, we must wonder how the example of Agabus should influence those churches that have adopted the teaching of *fallible prophecy.* Remember that Grudem presents three main components to Agabus' prophecy, *according to his interpretation: 1) the fact of Paul's arrest (true); 2) Paul being bound by the Jews (false); and 3) the Jews delivering Paul over to the Gentiles (false).* Yet we must note that Luke and the local residents did not respond to *what was erroneous,* but only to that which *was true:*

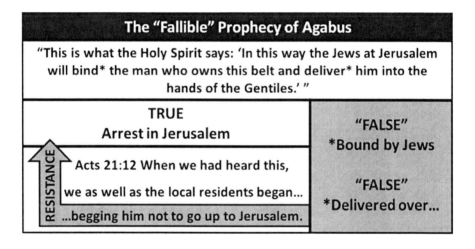

The "Fallible" Prophecy of Agabus

"This is what the Holy Spirit says: 'In this way the Jews at Jerusalem will bind* the man who owns this belt and deliver* him into the hands of the Gentiles.' "

TRUE Arrest in Jerusalem	"FALSE" *Bound by Jews
RESISTANCE — Acts 21:12 When we had heard this, we as well as the local residents began... ...begging him not to go up to Jerusalem.	"FALSE" *Delivered over...

The fact that Luke and the local residents offered *initial resistance*[138] to the core truth of this prophecy is a strange consequence of their *sifting*

---

[138] It is simply fallacious to assume that Luke's narrative in Acts reveals some form of error with respect to Agabus' prophecy, or that the initial resistance to his utterance was due to such supposed error. Writing by the leading of the Spirit, with the articulation of a careful historian, Luke's record reveals a strong affirmation of Agabus' veracity and authority as a genuine prophet of God. His familiarity with Agabus is evident in view of Acts 11:27-28 and Acts 21:10. In each text, Agabus is identified as a prophet. In view of this, if Agabus did err in Acts 21:10, then a historic correction from Luke's pen would be necessary, especially in view of Agabus' clear, indicative, and complete attribution to the Holy Spirit. Thus, Luke's silence is stunning in view of the presumptions of *fallible prophecy.* In

through what was said. Of course, one must wonder how they could discern and protest the supposed elements of error. For example, should they have sought to contradict Agabus' assertion about *how Paul would be bound*? If this were the case, we might wonder how they were supposed to know that it would be impossible for the Jews to bind Paul, as Grudem asserts. As well, should they have resisted the idea that the Jews *would deliver Paul over to the Romans*, and if so, how would they have known about this "error"?[139] After all, the Jews delivered Christ over, therefore, how could they have known that things would be different with Paul? There is no reason to assume that such resistance to Agabus' prophecy would have been intuitive, called for, or even reasonable. Remarkably, in all of Scripture we have the example of Agabus, whose *prophecy (the valid portion – Paul's* arrest) was resisted in view of the supposed erroneous elements contained within (*binding, delivering over*). Thus, as a central sample for modern day *fallible prophecy*, Agabus' example supplies an abundance of confusion. By the example of Ababus, along with those who responded to him, *no fallible prophecy would ever have to be honored or recognized for this simple reason: all fallible prophecies contain some error, by definition.* Exactly how could such

---

addition to this, Paul's silence is equally troubling in view of his instructions requiring strict scrutiny of the claimants of prophecy (1 Corinthians 14:29, 1 Thessalonians 5:20-22). Thus, Paul's lack of correction of Agabus' supposed errors constitutes a troubling disobedience to such commands. Finally, Luke reminds us that he, along with the local residents, ultimately surrendered themselves to what God revealed through Agabus after delivering their emotional appeals to Paul: "...since he would not be persuaded, we fell silent, remarking, 'The will of the Lord be done'" (Acts 21:14). Such a conclusion as this affirms Luke's recognition of Agabus' veracity and authority as God's messenger.

[139] Grudem asserts that Luke and the local residents should have suspected some of the weaknesses of Agabus' prophecy: "Probably anyone who knew how the Jews throughout the Empire had treated Paul in various cities could have 'predicted' with no revelation from the Holy Spirit at all that Paul would meet violent opposition from the Jews in Jerusalem. What was unique about Agabus's prophecy was this prediction of 'binding' and 'delivering into the hands of the Gentiles.' And on these two key elements, he is just a bit wrong." Grudem, The Gift of Prophecy, 79.

confusion be called *edification*, as Grudem and others suppose? As will be discussed in the conclusion of this book, *fallible prophecy* is more than a murky doctrine, it is spiritually dangerous. For a person to claim to have a direct revelation from God is serious enough; but to bind the conscience of other believers with errant declarations that are labeled as *prophecy*, is potentially devastating.

Yet we must query further. Amidst the morass of confusion and contradiction surrounding Agabus' *"fallible prophecy,"* the only moment of clarity and resolve that comes to Luke and the others is that which comes by the Apostle Paul. According to Grudem, this is presented to us by Luke in order to "show the contrast between Paul's sure knowledge of God's will...and the uncertain grasp of God's will possessed by the prophets and other disciples":[140]

> Acts 21:12–13: 12 When we had heard this, we as well as the local residents began begging him not to go up to Jerusalem. 13 Then Paul answered, "What are you doing, weeping and breaking my heart? For I am ready not only to be bound, but even to die at Jerusalem for the name of the Lord Jesus."

Several observations are in order concerning Grudem's interpretation of these passages: First, Paul's "sure knowledge" does not appear to include any clarity regarding the outcome of his arrest in Jerusalem. Though he was prepared to die in Jerusalem, *he would not die in Jerusalem.* In that sense, he did not know more than what was supplied by Agabus and his prophecy. Second, Agabus' prophecy offers no exhortation or prohibition to Paul, instead, the Spirit simply reveals to Paul the fact that he will be arrested as a result of his visit to Jerusalem. Yet, Grudem presumes that there is an implied message given by Agabus to Paul, one that is repeated by Luke and the local residents: *that Paul should not go to Jerusalem.* In very simple terms, the scriptural data does not support such a

---

[140] Ibid.

presumption. Third, if Luke's "point" is to show Paul's superior knowledge - a knowledge which rescues the people from the morass of their confusion and contradiction, then how is the New Testament church supposed to apply such an example? If a believer is presented with an *exhortative or predictive* utterance by a *fallible prophet,* resulting in uncertainty and confusion due to the presence of *any error,* then how will such a believer resolve such uncertainty without the presence of a living, breathing Apostle - *as Agabus, Luke, and the local residents had*? When we take the example of Agabus *at its face value,* we must wonder if God would provide the "gift of *fallible prophecy*" as a means of edification for the modern church, yet without the requisite oversight of living apostles. Without such apostolic oversight, where could we hope to find edification within the narrative of Acts 21, or especially in the modern day?

With all of this, *fallible prophecy's* principal example of a New Testament prophet is revealed to be a phantom and the use and application of Agabus' example is shown to be disastrous. How anyone could conclude that the church can derive edification from such matters is truly incredible. Yet, according to the advocates of *fallible prophecy,* this is a gift of God that continues in the modern church such that *nearly everyone* can exercise such a gift for the edification of God's people.

CHAPTER 4:

– FALLIBLE PROPHECY –

A GIFT FOR ALL?

Our examination of Agabus was lengthy, yet needful. Without Agabus, the advocates of *fallible prophecy* lose their most explicit, scriptural example of a New Testament prophet - one who is identified by Luke as a prophet, whose prophecy is directly attributed to the Holy Spirit, and whose utterance received important reactions from Paul, Luke, and several other disciples. Yet, Agabus is not the only basis for their position; several other passages are typically advanced within a broader, more implicit argument for *fallible prophecy.* Typically, there are a great number of passages that can be consulted on this subject, yet, only a few are significantly emphasized. When one looks at the history of the overall debate it is evident that certain adjustments and refinements have been made from both sides of the argument. In the earliest stages of the *fallible prophecy* debate, Ephesians 2:20 took center stage. In this verse, Grudem has argued that Paul's mention of *apostles and prophets* points not to two groups, but just one: *the apostles who are prophets.* Though Grudem still maintains this position, he has adjusted the dogmatism of his view:

"Some have argued that Ephesians 2:20 shows what all New Testament prophets were like, and, furthermore, that the unique 'foundational' role of the prophets in Ephesians 2:20 means that they could speak with authority equal to the apostles and equal to Scripture...The four most common interpretations of Ephesians 2:20 and 3:5 may be summarized as arguing that the phrase 'the foundation of the apostles and prophets' means: 1. the apostles and the Old Testament prophets, 2. the teaching of the apostles and New Testament prophets, 3. the apostles and New Testament prophets themselves, or, 4. the apostle-prophets themselves (that is, the apostles who are also prophets)... even if a reader did prefer, for example, view 3, it should not significantly affect the argument of the rest of this book. That is because I would simply respond that, if Ephesians 2:20 and 3:5 talk about two distinct groups, apostles and prophets, then the 'prophets' mentioned here would be those who share authority similar to the apostles-and they would therefore be unlike the ordinary prophets scattered throughout many early Christian congregations who are described in much more detail in other parts of the New Testament."[141]

There are multiple issues with Grudem's arguments surrounding Ephesians 2:20, not the least of which is his nuanced disjunction of Ephesians 4:11 from the context of Ephesians 2:20 and 3:5. Seeing that this issue has been adequately addressed by the aforementioned authors (Thomas, Farnell, Edgar, and Compton), we will look to other passages for our analysis of *fallible prophecy*, especially since Grudem is willing to allow for the dismissal of his preferred version of Ephesians 2:20. His willingness to do so is based upon his insistence that other, non-authoritative prophets "are described *in much more detail in other parts of the New Testament.*" Because of his stress on the strength of *other* passages, we will focus our attention on those texts which Grudem centrally utilizes for his proposition of *fallible prophecy*, namely, 1 Corinthians 14:5, 29, and 1 Thessalonians 5:21. Categorically speaking, Grudem favors these texts in the advancement of his view that New Testament Prophecy is: 1. Fallible/non-authoritative (1 Corinthians 14:29 [1 Thessalonians 5:21]); and 2. Extremely common (1 Corinthians 14:5). Of course, these are not the only passages utilized by Grudem but they do formulate the centerpiece of his *implicit* argument for *fallible prophecy*. As well, through our focus on these three core passages, we will also consider other related texts which Grudem utilizes in support of his thesis. Because of Grudem's emphasis on Paul's first epistle to the Corinthians, we will pursue our study in two major sections: *1. Paul's broader ministry to the Corinthians, and 2. Key exegetical problems within 1 Corinthians and other texts.*

Paul's Broader Ministry to the Corinthians

As we delve into 1 Corinthians 14, we must first make sure that we understand Paul's broader ministry to the church at Corinth. Failure to

---

[141] Grudem, The Gift of Prophecy, 45-47.

do this would leave us bereft of the important context of Paul's efforts to minister to a deeply troubled church. Without such a broader context, we may confuse or conflate Paul's *prescriptions* to the church with his *descriptions* of their problematic conduct. Most of what Paul wrote to the church was corrective in nature. This is even evident in references to his lost epistles. Overall, Paul wrote *four epistles* to Corinth, two of which we have today within the canon of Scripture. His two non-canonical letters are mentioned as follows:

1. Paul's first letter (prior to 1 Corinthians): Though we do not have this epistle, Paul does give us brief insight into one important aspect of his teaching to the church: "I wrote you in my letter not to associate with immoral people..." 1 Corinthians 5:9. The context of this reference in 1 Corinthians pertains to Paul's rebuke against the church's toleration of sin. Thus, from his initial letter to 1 Corinthians it is evident that the church failed to make adequate progress concerning their pursuit of purity in the church.

2. The sorrowful letter (prior to 2 Corinthians): This letter reveals Paul's anguish over the needed progress of the Corinthian church. It is often referred to as the *sorrowful letter*: "For out of much affliction and anguish of heart I wrote to you with many tears; not so that you would be made sorrowful, but that you might know the love which I have especially for you" 2 Corinthians 2:4. Once again, we see evidences of Paul's agonizing pursuit for the Corinthians' progress in their sanctification.

When we survey all of Paul's instructions to the Corinthians, it becomes quite evident that his love and concern for this assembly was great. He labored in their midst from the beginning, ministering the word to them for one and a half years (Acts 18:1-17). In the introduction of 1 Corinthians Paul expressed thanks to God for their better beginning[142] as

---

[142] The Corinthians had been given an abundance of grace whereby *they were enriched* [*eploutisthēte*] in all speech and all knowledge. Paul utilizes the Aorist verb in order to give them a snapshot reminder of their beginnings as a church: they had been given God's

a church, reminding them that, in Christ, they had been enriched "in all speech and all knowledge" (1 Corinthians 1:5). Having been an eyewitness to their beginning, Paul became increasingly distressed in view of their downgrade over time such that his epistles, 1st and 2nd Corinthians, are filled with an abundance of corrections, rebukes, and warnings in addition to his general instructions. The following is a summary of his *corrections, rebukes, and warnings* given to the Corinthians:

- **1 Corinthians 1:** Paul had been informed that divisions were developing in Corinth. – verse 10: *"Now I exhort you, brethren, by the name of our Lord Jesus Christ, that you all agree and that there be no divisions among you, but that you be made complete in the same mind and in the same judgment."*

- **1 Corinthians 3:** Paul continues his refutation of the divisions that were growing at Corinth in verses 1–3: *1 And I, brethren, could not speak to you as to spiritual men, but as to men of flesh, as to infants in Christ. 2 I gave you milk to drink, not solid food; for you were not yet able to receive it. Indeed, even now you are not yet able, 3 for you are still fleshly. For since there is jealousy and strife among you, are you not fleshly, and are you not walking like mere men?*

- **1 Corinthians 4:** Paul *admonishes* the Corinthians (v. 14) in light of their premature judgment of his leadership as an Apostle – verses 3 & 5: *3 But to me it is a very small thing that I may be examined by you, or by any human court; in fact, I do not even examine myself... 5 Therefore do not go on passing judgment before the time.*

- **1 Corinthians 5:** As a follow-up to his unheeded warnings in the "lost letter," Paul rebukes the church for their toleration of the man who was engaged in overt immorality – verses 1–2: *1 It is actually reported that there is immorality among you, and immorality of such a kind as does not*

---

genuine knowledge rather than the counterfeit "wisdom" of the world (1 Corinthians 1:18-31).

exist even among the Gentiles, that someone has his father's wife. 2 You have become arrogant and have not mourned instead, so that the one who had done this deed would be removed from your midst.

- **1 Corinthians 6:** Paul exposes the shame of their litigious conduct and immoral practices in worship – verses 5-6, 15: *5 I say this to your shame... 6...brother goes to law with brother, and that before unbelievers?...15 Do you not know that your bodies are members of Christ? Shall I then take away the members of Christ and make them members of a prostitute? May it never be!*

- **1 Corinthians 8:** Paul speaks against the Corinthians' arrogance (v. 1) with regard to their reckless sense of Christian liberty – verse 12: *And so, by sinning against the brethren and wounding their conscience when it is weak, you sin against Christ.*

- **1 Corinthians 9:** Paul actually had to defend his calling as an Apostle of Jesus Christ – verse 1: *1 Am I not free? Am I not an apostle? Have I not seen Jesus our Lord? Are you not my work in the Lord?*

- **1 Corinthians 10:** Paul warns them concerning the paganizing influences of the world and, again, confronts their flagrant sense of liberty – verses 21 & 23: *21 You cannot drink the cup of the Lord and the cup of demons; you cannot partake of the table of the Lord and the table of demons...23 All things are lawful, but not all things are profitable. All things are lawful, but not all things edify.*

- **1 Corinthians 11-14:** Paul rebukes elements of their disorderly and self-serving conduct found within their practices of corporate worship, beginning with their deadly[143] abuse of the Lord's table – verses 11:20–21:

---

[143] The abuses of the Lord's table had become so excessive that Paul mentions God's judgment upon them for these repeated indiscretions: 1 Corinthians 11:30–31: 30 For this reason many among you are weak and sick, and a number sleep. 31 But if we judged ourselves rightly, we would not be judged.

20 Therefore when you meet together, it is not to eat the Lord's Supper, 21 for in your eating each one takes his own supper first; and one is hungry and another is drunk. He then addresses their "ignorance" concerning spiritual gifts – verses 12:3: *3 Therefore I make known to you that no one speaking by the Spirit of God says, "Jesus is accursed"; and no one can say, "Jesus is Lord," except by the Holy Spirit.* He teaches that with any potential service or aspect of giftedness, Christ-like love must be foremost in everything – verse: *13:2 If I have the gift of prophecy, and know all mysteries and all knowledge; and if I have all faith, so as to remove mountains, but do not have love, I am nothing.* And he reminds them that, in all things, our worship must be orderly because God is not the author of confusion – verses 14:40 & 33: *40 But all things must be done properly and in an orderly manner... 33...God is not a God of confusion but of peace, as in all the churches of the saints.*

- **1 Corinthians 15:** Paul eviscerates those who were teaching false doctrines which denied the resurrection – verses 12–17: *12 Now if Christ is preached, that He has been raised from the dead, how do some among you say that there is no resurrection of the dead? 13 But if there is no resurrection of the dead, not even Christ has been raised; 14 and if Christ has not been raised, then our preaching is vain, your faith also is vain. 15 Moreover we are even found to be false witnesses of God, because we testified against God that He raised Christ, whom He did not raise, if in fact the dead are not raised. 16 For if the dead are not raised, not even Christ has been raised; 17 and if Christ has not been raised, your faith is worthless; you are still in your sins.*

- **1 Corinthians 16:** Having given his excellent treatise on love in chapter 13, Paul seals his epistle with an exhortation and severe warning regarding the centrality of love in everything – verses 14 & 22: *14 Let all that you do be done in love...22 If anyone does not love the Lord, he is to be accursed. Maranatha.*

This brief summary gives us a very important sense of context for the whole of 1 Corinthians, and Paul's closing exhortations concerning love offer an essential capstone. As we considered in the first chapter, 1 Corinthians 16:22 offers a stunning yet fitting conclusion to Paul's warnings and instructions to the Corinthians, especially when we consider his strong emphasis on the centrality of love in 1 Corinthians 13. Such an emphasis on love is so important, in fact, that we should give it more attention before proceeding further. In the modern day, we often see the contents of 1 Corinthians 13 on decorative placards, picture frames, and refrigerator magnets. Yet, as beautiful as this chapter is, it stands in tandem with Paul's grave warning at the conclusion of the entire epistle: *if anyone does not love the Lord, he is to be accursed.* Paul's continuity of emphasis on love in this letter is deeply profound. Moreover, the fact that he utilizes the word *philos* rather than *agape* in this final warning is remarkably instructive. We are reminded of the distinction of these words *via* Christ's last exchange with Peter before His ascension into heaven:

> John 21:15–17: 15 So when they had finished breakfast, Jesus said to Simon Peter, "Simon, son of John, do you love [*agapas*] Me more than these?" He said to Him, "Yes, Lord; You know that I love [*philo*] You." He said to him, "Tend My lambs." 16 He said to him again a second time, "Simon, son of John, do you love [*agapas*] Me?" He said to Him, "Yes, Lord; You know that I love [*philo*] You." He said to him, "Shepherd My sheep." 17 He said to him the third time, "Simon, son of John, do you love [*phileis*] Me?" Peter was grieved because He said to him the third time, "Do you love [*phileis*] Me?" And he said to Him, "Lord, You know all things; You know that I love [*philo*] You." Jesus said to him, "Tend My sheep.

Peter's use of *philo*, in contrast to Christ's use of *agape*, is very significant. The Savior's repeated use of *agape* reveals His desire for the higher bond of love; however, Peter's responses revealed a more general expression of human affection. The fact that this exchange took place three times recalls to mind Peter's threefold denial of the Savior. In this final exchange before His ascension, Christ graciously condescended to

Peter's own expression in order to extend His mercy and grace to one whose frailty and weakness had become so evident before all, as William Hendrikson notes:

> "With becoming modesty and pleasing diffidence Peter, humiliated by the memory of his fall, refuses to use the higher term for love, the verb which Jesus had used. For the love of intelligence and purpose, the love of whole-hearted devotion, about which Jesus was asking, Peter substitutes the more subjective *affection*."[144]

Such a comparison of terms for love is helpful for our own study. Paul's use of *philōs* in 1 Corinthians 16:22 represents a more basic form of love than *agapē*. For a frail, weak, and stumbling church, Paul's warning was crucial. Christians are called to love [*agapas*] the Lord God in view of the foremost commandment; yet if the more primitive affection of *philos* is absent, then the *supposed worshipper* is nothing more than an accursed soul: like those whose joy is centered in the gifts of Christ rather than in Christ and His kingdom above all (Matthew 7:22-23). In view of these matters, we should remember that Paul wasn't merely concerned that there were those in their ranks who were making foolish mistakes; he was most deeply concerned that there were those whose religious activities amounted to nothing more than a Christless and loveless religious-hysteria, worthy of the eternal anathema of God.[145] For others, he was

---

[144] William Hendriksen, <u>New Testament Commentary: Exposition of the Gospel According to John</u>, (Grand Rapids, Michigan: Baker Book House, 1958), 487.

[145] Matthew Henry weighs in on this piercing text: 1 Cor 16:22 – "With a very solemn warning to them: If any man love not the Lord Jesus Christ, let him be Anathema, Maranatha, v. 22. We sometimes need words of threatening, that we may fear. Blessed is he, says the wise man, who feareth always. Holy fear is a very good friend both to holy faith and holy living. An how much reason have all Christians to fear falling under this doom! If any man love not the Lord Jesus Christ, let him be Anathema, Maran-atha. Here observe, 1. The person described, who is liable to this doom: He that loveth not the Lord Jesus Christ. A meiosis, as some think; he who blasphemes Christ disowns his doctrine, slights and contemns his institutions, or, through pride of human knowledge and learning, despises

concerned that they were being led astray like naive children, carried about by every wind of doctrine. This same concern of his was repeated in his instructions on the gifts of the Spirit:

1 Corinthians 3:1: And I, brethren, could not speak to you as to spiritual men, but as to men of flesh, as to infants in Christ.

1 Corinthians 14:20: Brethren, do not be children in your thinking; yet in evil be infants, but in your thinking be mature.

---

his revelations. It stands here as a warning to the Corinthians and a rebuke of their criminal behaviour. It is an admonition to them not to be led away from the simplicity of the gospel, or those principles of it which were the great motives to purity of life, by pretenders to science, by the wisdom of the world, which would call their religion folly, and its most important doctrines absurd and ridiculous. Those men had a spite at Christ; and, if the Corinthians give ear to their seducing speeches, they were in danger of apostatizing from him. Against this he gives them here a very solemn caution. "Do not give into such conduct, if you would escape the severest vengeance.' ' Note, Professed Christians will, by contempt of Christ, and revolt from him, bring upon themselves the most dreadful destruction. Some understand the words as they lie, in their plain and obvious meaning, for such as are without holy and sincere affection for the Lord Jesus Christ. Many who have his name much in their mouths have no true love to him in their hearts, will not have him to rule over them (Lu. 19:27), no, not though they have very towering hopes of being saved by him. And none love him in truth who do not love his laws and keep his commandments. Note, There are many Christians in name who do not love Christ Jesus the Lord in sincerity. But can any thing be more criminal or provoking? What, not love the most glorious lover in the world! Him who loved us, and gave himself for us, who shed his blood for us, to testify his love to us, and that after heinous wrong and provocation! What had we a power of loving for, if we are unmoved with such love as this, and without affection to such a Saviour? But, 2. We have here the doom of the person described: "Let him be Anathema, Maran-atha, lie under the heaviest and most dreadful curse. Let him be separated from the people of God, from the favour of God, and delivered up to his final, irrevocable, and inexorable vengeance'" Henry, M. (1994). Matthew Henry's commentary on the whole Bible: Complete and unabridged in one volume (1 Co 16:19–24). Peabody: Hendrickson.

Without this broader context of Paul's ministry to the Corinthians, we could run the risk of presuming too much about Paul's prescriptions and descriptions in his writings. For example, as a pastor I have had people approach me with passages like 1 Corinthians 14:26, insisting that the church should assemble and worship after the Corinthian pattern:

> 1 Corinthians 14:26: What is the outcome then, brethren? When you assemble, each one has a psalm, has a teaching, has a revelation, has a tongue, has an interpretation. Let all things be done for edification.

Unfortunately, there are those who assume that Paul's mere *description* of the Corinthians' activities should be received as an affirmation of their conduct and thus be applied as a *prescription* for the whole body of Christ; yet such thinking is exegetically reckless. Instead, we should remember the broader context of Paul's instructions to the Corinthians. In chapter 12 Paul supplied a very rudimentary lesson on spiritual gifts, beginning with his concern over their ignorance - *"Now concerning spiritual gifts, brethren, I would not have you ignorant" (verse 1).* Paul then continues with his description of the Spirit's sovereign distribution of gifts, saying, *"All are not teachers are they?...All do not speak with tongues, do they? All do not interpret, do they?"* (1 Corinthians 12:29-30). When comparing Paul's rudimentary lessons in chapter 12 with his description of the Corinthian's conduct in chapter 14, it becomes quite evident that the church was dramatically overestimating its true giftedness. The result of such conduct was severe disorder and a loss of *genuine edification.* The connecting chapter on love[146] (chapter 13) reminds us that their errors were not superficial, but deeply dangerous seeing that they were not operating out of a Christ-centered love. Though there are some evidences

---

[146] The connectedness of chapter 13 to Paul's teaching on spiritual gifts (chapters 12 & 14) is quite evident: 1 Corinthians 12:31: "But earnestly desire the greater gifts. And I show you a still more excellent way... " Chapter 13 (the supremacy and excellence of love) ... 1 Corinthians 14:1: "Pursue love, yet desire earnestly spiritual gifts, but especially that you may prophesy."

of later progress in 2 Corinthians,[147] the Apostle's great concern for many in their midst continued with alarming severity in view of the following:

1. Their *Continued* Acceptance of False Messengers and False Gospels - 2 Corinthians 11:3–4, 13-15: *3 But I am afraid that, as the serpent deceived Eve by his craftiness, your minds will be led astray from the simplicity and purity of devotion to Christ. 4 For if one comes and preaches another Jesus whom we have not preached, or you receive a different spirit which you have not received, or a different gospel which you have not accepted, you bear this beautifully... 13 For such men are false apostles, deceitful workers, disguising themselves as apostles of Christ. 14 No wonder, for even Satan disguises himself as an angel of light. 15 Therefore it is not surprising if his servants also disguise themselves as servants of righteousness, whose end will be according to their deeds.*

2. Their Dangerous Resistance to Apostolic Authority - 2 Corinthians 12:19–20a: *19 All this time you have been thinking that we are defending ourselves to you. Actually, it is in the sight of God that we have been speaking in Christ; and all for your upbuilding, beloved. 20 For I am afraid that perhaps when I come I may find you to be not what I wish and may be found by you to be not what you wish...*

3. Their Fleshly, Arrogant, and Divisive Behavior - 2 Corinthians 12:20b–21: *20b ...that perhaps there will be strife, jealousy, angry tempers, disputes, slanders, gossip, arrogance, disturbances; 21 I am afraid that when I come again my God may humiliate me before you, and I may mourn over many of those who have sinned in the past and not repented of the impurity, immorality and sensuality which they have practiced.*

4. The Grave Questions Raised by their Repeated Rebellion - 2 Corinthians 13:5–6: *5 Test yourselves to see if you are in the faith; examine yourselves! Or do you not recognize this about yourselves, that Jesus Christ is in you—unless indeed you fail the test? 6 But I trust that you will realize that we ourselves do not fail the test.*

---

[147] See especially, 2 Corinthians 2 & 7.

Paul's concern for the Corinthians was deep and rooted in genuine love, and for this reason he was willing to say difficult things to a stubborn assembly. The voluminous nature of his warnings to the Corinthians should remind us to take great care when seeking to interpret and apply the Apostle's *descriptions* and *prescriptions* supplied within his letters. Moreover, what he writes should warn us in the present day about the church's use and application of the Spirit's gifts, remembering that *spiritual presumption is a very dangerous thing*. Though the Corinthians believed themselves to be *a remarkably gifted church*, their spiritual trajectory belied their presumptions. Their deviations revealed, not the fruit of the Spirit (the chief fruit of which is love), but the bad fruit of fleshliness, worldly wisdom, impurity, immorality, and sensuality.

Key Exegetical Problems

With these contextual considerations in place, we will now proceed with an analysis of Grudem's interpretation of passages from 1 Corinthians. As we do, I should also state that our central focus will be on the subject at hand: *fallible prophecy*. Thus, a thorough treatment of 1 Corinthians 11-14 is beyond the scope of this work, so our studies will need to focus on Grudem's most central treatment of the subject of prophecy. We will begin with two different translations of 1 Corinthians 14:5, the latter of which Grudem utilizes heavily in his writings:

NASB - 1 Corinthians 14:5: 5 Now I wish [*thelō*] that you all spoke in tongues, but even more that you would prophesy; and greater is one who prophesies than one who speaks in tongues, unless he interprets, so that the church may receive edifying.

ESV - 1 Corinthians 14:5 Now I want [*thelō*] you all to speak in tongues, but even more to prophesy. The one who prophesies is greater than the one who speaks in tongues, unless someone interprets, so that the church may be built up.

The differences between these translations must be carefully considered since the distinction between the renderings of *thelō* (*wish* vs. *want*) is quite significant. Grudem utilizes the latter translation (*thelō* as *want*) and repeatedly asserts that Paul *wanted* all the Corinthians to speak in tongues and, even more so, to prophecy:

> "Another great benefit of prophecy is that it provides opportunity for participation by *everyone* in the congregation, not just those who are skilled speakers or who have gifts of teaching. Paul says that he wants 'all' the Corinthians to prophesy (1 Cor. 14:5)..."[148]

Grudem argues from this verse and others that the gift of New Testament prophecy was (and is) extremely common, making it distinguishable from the authoritative prophecy found in the Old Testament. How Grudem is able to make these quantifications is left to the imagination of the reader.[149] Yet Grudem presses this notion of a *common gift of prophecy*; one that was fallible and non-authoritative; one which Paul *wanted all* to pursue and utilize (1 Corinthians 14:5). The inherent contradiction to such a view should be self-evident. As mentioned before, Paul sought to correct the Corinthians' presumptions about the extent of their giftedness whereby he said, "all are not teachers are they?...all do not speak with tongues, do they? All do not interpret, do they?" (1 Corinthians 12:29-30). Since it is the case that *not all* speak in tongues or prophecy, then why would Paul want *all* the Corinthians to pursue what the Lord would not supply? Such a thought is utterly irreconcilable. However, the NASB translators have captured the right sense of Paul's expression: "Now I

---

[148] Grudem, The Gift of Prophecy, 324, italics mine.

[149] "...the gift of prophecy functioned...in thousands of ordinary Christians in hundreds of local churches at the time of the New Testament...the words 'prophet' and 'prophecy' are used more commonly to refer to ordinary Christians who spoke not with absolute divine authority but simply to report something that God had brought to their minds..." Ibid., 286.

wish [*thelō*] that you all spoke in tongues." Like other words in the Old and New Testament Scriptures, *thelō* is a word whose semantic domain allows for varying connotations *depending on the context.* In our case the context of 1 Corinthians 14:5 correlates strongly with 1 Corinthians 7:7-8 where Paul says:

> "Yet I wish [*thelō*] that all men were even as I myself am. However, each man has his own gift from God, one in this manner, and another in that." 8 "But I say to the unmarried and to widows that it is good for them if they remain even as I."[150]

In this section, Paul is responding to a question posited by the Corinthians about the benefits of singleness: "Now concerning the things about which you wrote, it is good for a man not to touch a woman..." (1 Corinthians 1:1). The apparent problem in Corinth was that some were pressing the benefit of singleness to a fault such that some were seeking to justify the dissolution of the marital union; but Paul refuted such extreme thinking and gave the injunction: "Are you bound to a wife? Do not seek to be released. Are you released from a wife? Do not seek a wife. But if you marry, you have not sinned..." (1 Corinthians 7:27-28). Paul's instructions on singleness and marriage in 1 Corinthians 7 gives us an important understanding of the benefits of singleness and the covenant obligations of marriage. Paul did not want the church to view the benefits of singleness to the extent that they would dishonor the institution of marriage, but he did want the church to consider the benefits of singleness "in view of the present distress" (1 Corinthians 7:26) of persecution. Ultimately, Paul's *wish* that all were even as he was (single) is subsequently qualified by his recognition of the Lord's sovereign distribution of gifts, according to His will. For Paul to *wish* that others could enjoy the benefits of singleness was not an attempt to subvert God's sovereign distribution of giftedness. Paul's ultimate instructions

---

[150] NASB, italics mine.

correspond with what the Savior said to the disciples after they expressed the benefits of singleness:

> Matthew 19:10b–12: 10 "...it is better not to marry." 11 But He said to them, "Not all men can accept this statement, but only those to whom it has been given. 12 "For there are eunuchs who were born that way from their mother's womb; and there are eunuchs who were made eunuchs by men; and there are also eunuchs who made themselves eunuchs for the sake of the kingdom of heaven. He who is able to accept this, let him accept it."

For Paul to *wish* that all could be single is a simple statement of *hypothetical musing* rather than an *exhortative injunction*. However, if we were to accept Paul's expression in 1 Corinthians 7:7 as an *injunction*, then the Apostle would be guilty of instructing all the brethren at Corinth to pursue singleness in direct violation of his subsequent recognition of God's sovereign distribution of the gift of singleness. 1 Corinthians 7:7 supplies a strong parallel to 1 Corinthians 14:5. Paul's *wish* that all the Corinthians could speak in tongues and prophesy is clearly an expression of *hypothetical musing* in light of his former reminder that "all are not prophets..." and "all do not speak with tongues." As he already stated, *each one is given the manifestation of the Spirit for the common good.* In other words, it is not about what Paul or the Corinthians *wanted*, but what the Lord wills for His people. For Paul to say that he *wished* that all the Corinthians could speak in tongues and prophecy is consistent with the manner in which he instructed and corrected the church. At the beginning of the epistle, Paul reminded the church that they were "not lacking in any gift" (1 Corinthians 1:7). For those who falsely believed that *each member* had the gift of teaching; the gift of revelation, of tongues, and the interpretation of tongues, this was a needful reminder. As already mentioned, Paul later refutes the false notion that each member of the body could have all the gifts (1 Corinthians 12:28-30), thereby reminding them that it is the Spirit who sovereignly supplies such gifts *for the common good* (1 Corinthians 12:7) and no member should be jealous or discontent over the Spirit's sovereign distribution of such gifts (1 Corinthians 12:14-26). Such correctives would have been massive to a church that had grossly overestimated its giftedness and it would be wrong for them to conclude that they were thereby lacking in what they *truly needed* according to God's sovereign provision. Therefore, Paul's statement that he *wished* they all could speak in tongues and prophecy (as they falsely believed) was his way of *heralding the value of the gifts, the greatest of which was prophecy.* This corresponds to Paul's *hypothetical wish* that the Corinthians could enjoy the benefits of unfettered ministry *via* singleness. However, if we were to take these expressions as *exhortative injunctions,* then we would inherit an abundance of doctrinal confusion. The problem at Corinth was that they did believe that the gifts of the Spirit were common provisions to all – so common that, when they assembled, *each member sought to exercise their supposed "gift."* It is for this reason that Paul applies restraints on their practices, requiring two or three speakers to proceed with the requisite judgment and interpretation that prophecy and tongues requires. Without such restraints and control, their worship was reduced to utter confusion; but Paul's instructions had the design of honoring the One who *is not the author of confusion* (1 Corinthians 14:33). Sadly, the church's practice revealed a desire for self-edification, rather than mutual edification within the body of Christ. Some sought to exercise their genuine gifts of the Spirit for the common good, while others desired to edify themselves by means of their *presumed* giftedness. This division between those who sought the common good of the body versus those who sought their own desires permeated all aspects of their worship, especially the Lord's table. Corinth's *bacchanalian* abuses of the Lord's Table resulted in the sickness and death of "many" in their midst (1 Corinthians 11:23-31).[151] Thus, there were factions within their ranks between those who sought to do

---

[151] Paul used the word many (*polloi*) to describe the extent to which the Lord's table was being abused: 1 Corinthians 11:30–31: 30 For this reason many among you are weak and sick, and a number sleep. 31 But if we judged ourselves rightly, we would not be judged.

God's will versus those who sought out their own desires in their corporate assembly. These factions, Paul said, were necessary so that *those who were approved would become evident* among the flock; and wherever the genuine gifts of the Spirit were manifested, they were to be desired and sought out earnestly within their assembly (1 Corinthians 14:1). Corinth was not lacking what they *actually needed* (1 Corinthians 1:7), but neither were they as endowed as many falsely presumed (1 Corinthians 12:29-30; 14:26). Their self-deception yielded an abundance of confusion and sapped the church of needed edification. Those who claimed to have the gifts of the Spirit, especially prophecy, did so with little accountability. Since their habit was to ignore God's prescribed tests of love for any claimant of prophecy, Paul instructed them in a *better way*:

> NASB - 1 Corinthians 14:29: Let two or three prophets speak, and let the others pass judgment [*diakrinetōsan*].

Corinth's tolerance of those who uttered blasphemies in the name of the Holy Spirit (1 Corinthians 12:3) was inexcusable, and failure to apply the scriptural tests to the claimant of prophecy revealed an absence of genuine love (Deuteronomy 13:1-5, 1 Corinthians 13). Corinth's unwillingness to reject grave error in their midst was a festering disease and would not be tolerated by the Apostle Paul. Thus, 1 Corinthians 14:29 supplied a needful prescription to a church that had been operating with no credible restraints. All of this should be clear enough to the reader, however, Grudem sees a different message in 1 Corinthians 14:29. For him, this text supplies essential proof for a legitimate, yet fallible gift of prophecy; one that was common and could be potentially exercised by *all* in the church. Commenting on this passage, Grudem asserts the following:

> "When Paul says, 'Let two or three prophets speak, and let the others weigh what is said" (1 Cor. 14:29), he suggests that they should listen carefully and sift the good from the bad, accepting some and rejecting the rest (for this is the

implication of the Greek words *diakrinō*, here translated 'weigh what is said'). We cannot imagine that an Old Testament prophet like Isaiah would have said, 'Listen to what I say and weigh what is said-sort the good from the bad, what you accept from what you should not accept'! If prophecy had absolute divine authority, it would be sin to do this. But here Paul commands that it be done, suggesting that New Testament prophecy did not have the authority of God's very words."[152]

Grudem's repeated use of this text is simply stunning. In his book, *The Gift of Prophecy in the New Testament and Today,* he manages to refer to this passage *72 times.* Such repetition reveals his dependency upon his interpretation of this one passage. Grudem assumes that Paul's use of the word *diakrinō* eliminates the idea of passing judgment over the *claimant of prophecy.* He believes that this is the case in view of his stress on an interpretation of *diakrinō* whereby a partitive analysis of the prophecy is in view only, *but not the prophet.* Yet, as we examined in *Chapter 1: Prophecy – A Test of Love,* the principal means by which any prophet was evaluated was through the passing of judgment *of what was said.* Therefore, the concept of a *partitive* analysis of a prophetic utterance does nothing to advance the thinking of *fallible prophecy.* Grudem's resistance to the notion of judging *the claimant of prophecy* has no scriptural basis, yet he offers not much more than a farcical offer by Isaiah: "Listen to what I say and weigh what is said-sort the good from the bad, what you accept from what you should not accept." Indeed, Isaiah would never say, *sort the good from the bad,* for a simple reason: he was a genuine prophet of God. However, this does not mean that Isaiah would have resisted critical evaluation as a prophet, for this would have been a contradiction to God's word as we have already examined in Deuteronomy 13:1-5, 18:18-22, and Jeremiah 14:13-15. The need for prophetic testing is rooted in the presence of *false prophets*, not genuine ones. A genuine prophet will always withstand scrutiny, but the false

---

[152] Grudem, <u>Systematic Theology</u>, 1054.

prophet will fail when evaluated by God's prescribed tests. What Grudem resists is the idea that the scrutiny prescribed in 1 Corinthians 14:29 is in any way similar to the Old Testament standard whereby the prophet was principally scrutinized by the accuracy or inaccuracy of his utterance. For him it would be sin to scrutinize an infallible messenger like Isaiah. Yet, the Apostle Paul was willing to subject himself to scrutiny over his own words:

> Galatians 1:8: But even if we, or an angel from heaven, should preach to you a gospel contrary to what we have preached to you, he is to be accursed!

Critical analysis and testing are absolute necessities for the body of Christ. Paul's willingness to be scrutinized demonstrates the need for the church to be discerning, and it also demonstrates the primacy of the message over the messenger.[153] When the Bereans heard the word of God through the Apostle Paul, they examined what he said by the standard of God's word. Rather than calling this sin or rebellion, Luke called the Bereans *noble-minded:*

> Acts 17:11: Now these were more noble-minded than those in Thessalonica, for they received the word with great eagerness, examining the Scriptures daily to see whether these things were so.

As an Apostle of Jesus Christ, Paul's message to the Bereans carried absolute authority, yet the Bereans scrutinized his words by the standard of Scripture. Such scrutiny was necessary for anyone claiming to be an Apostle or Prophet. When scriptural tests are applied, the genuine messengers of God have nothing to fear; but those who speak the *deception of their own minds* (Jeremiah 14:14) should tremble beneath such an evaluation. However, Grudem wants the church to accept a form of prophecy that offers a blend of truth and error. To his mind, sorting

---

[153] Galatians 2:11-21.

through the words and sayings of a prophecy means that the claimant of prophecy should still be accepted as a genuine prophet, despite the fact that *some error* comes from their lips. Such an interpretation of 1 Corinthians 14:29 is simply unjustified.[154] This reveals the crucial difference between *fallible prophecy* and the scriptural model: in the Old Testament, God's people were to sift through and sort out what a prophet said in order to determine the veracity or error of what was declared. If God truly spoke through the prophet, no error would be present. However, many false prophets delivered an admixture of truth and error which required careful judgment and analysis from the congregation. Like the prophets in Jeremiah 14, who spoke in the name of the Lord, their utterances were revealed to be corrupted because they were speaking the deception of their own minds. The false prophet who spoke in the name of God, with various utterances of truth about Him, would not be acquitted thereby. Simply put, 1 Corinthians 14:29 says nothing about *accepting* a presumed prophet despite the presence of error. What Paul did assert in this passage is the need for discernment to be applied to *anyone who thinks he is a prophet*, so as to determine the message (1 Corinthians 14:29), motive (1 Corinthians 13), and spirit (1 Corinthians 14:32) of the claimant of the prophetic gift. In light of Corinth's remarkable flirtations with errorists, they were clearly not applying such tests of love and discernment. Grudem's straw-man argument presumes too much from the text of 1 Corinthians 14:29 while failing to address the fact that Paul was looking to guide the Corinthians through the important

---

[154] With or without Grudem's connotation of *diakrinō*, the analogy of Scripture offers him no aid to the idea of accepting an *errorist* as a *genuine prophet*. There are other issues and problems concerning Grudem's interpretation of *diakrinō*, as Edgar notes: "...Carson's and Grudem's statements about the meaning of *diakrinō*...have little basis in fact. In the New Testament it can also mean to judge or evaluate people. In fact, it is used earlier in this epistle (1 Corinthians 6:5) in the same way as in the Septuagint (see, e.g., Exod. 18:16; 1 Kings 3:9; Zech. 3:7 and many other passages in the Old Testament). If there is any sifting out, it is only in order to pass judgment regarding the persons being judged." Edgar, Satisfied by the Promise of the Spirit, 80.

process of adjudicating true prophets versus false prophets *by the standard of God's divine revelation:*

> 1 Corinthians 14:37: If anyone thinks[155] he is a prophet or spiritual, let him recognize that the things which I write to you are the Lord's commandment.

This passage supplies yet another reminder of Corinth's overestimation of its giftedness. Moreover, their failure to test (1 Corinthians 14:29) and adjudicate (1 Corinthians 14:37) the claimants of revelation was leading them into dangerous territory of false teaching and rebellion against God's authority. Their inability to discern error like, "Jesus is accursed" (1 Corinthians 12:3), or those who denied the resurrection of the dead (1 Corinthians 15:12), revealed their lack of resolve to "test the spirits" in their midst. By the time of the writing of 2 Corinthians, it was evident that the church was gladly accepting Satan's disguised *servants of righteousness* as if they were messengers of truth. It is this failure to reject *false messengers* in view of their *false message* that was plaguing the church. They were not judging the claimants of spiritual gifts rightly and this was opening the door to heretical thinking:

> 1 Corinthians 12:3: Therefore I make known to you that no one speaking by the Spirit of God says, "Jesus is accursed"; and no one can say, "Jesus is Lord," except by the Holy Spirit.

In this passage Paul makes it clear that much can be known about a speaker in view of what they say: "...no one speaking by the Spirit of God says, 'Jesus *is* accursed." His point is quite simple and clear: whatever the professed gift may be, an utterance is not attributable to the Holy Spirit *if the utterance is false.* It is important to note that Paul's judgment of the individual depends upon his partitive assessment of what they said. This expression, *Jesus is accursed,* is more primitive in the Greek. The normal

---

[155] G. *dokei – present active indicative of dokeō: to be of an opinion, to suppose.*

assumption is that the construction is elliptical in form such that the linking verb is merely assumed: (*Anathema Iēsous*) Jesus *is* accursed. As already discussed, this word accursed (*anathĕma*) is the same one used by Paul in his conclusive warning to the church: *If anyone does not love the Lord, let him be accursed (1 Corinthians 16:22)*. Clearly, without the Lord and His propitiation, we are all accursed. Yet, why wouldn't the error of 1 Corinthians 12:3 be immediately evident to the assembly at Corinth? Why would it be necessary for Paul to clarify such a problematic statement? We should remember that Paul elsewhere taught that Christ *did become a curse for us*:

> Galatians 3:13: Christ redeemed us from the curse of the Law, having become a curse for us—for it is written, "CURSED IS EVERYONE WHO HANGS ON A TREE"—

In this verse, Paul cites Deuteronomy 21:23 reminding us that the central reality of the Gospel is the fact that Christ became a curse for us as our sacrificial substitute. To an infantile church like Corinth, the differences between Galatians 3:13 and 1 Corinthians 12:3 might not have been immediately evident. However, the clarity of Galatians 3:13 leaves nothing to the human imagination. To the Galatians, Paul says that Christ *became* (*genomenos*) a curse (*katara*)[156] for us. Paul's use of the aorist participle, *genomenos*, points to Christ's historic and sufficient work on the Cross. When Christ said "it is finished" on the cross (John 19:30), He declared the absolute completion of His penal substitution on behalf of His sheep. Though Jesus *was* accursed there is no sense in which he *is* accursed in the present day. A modern expression of such erroneous thinking in 1 Corinthians 12:3 is found within the Roman Catholic teaching of

---

[156] Though the English word *curse* is used in both texts, the Greek words are different: *anathema (1 Corinthians 12:3)* and *katara (Galatians 3:13)*. Though Paul uses both terms to speak of God's judgment of mankind (*anathema*: 1 Corinthians 16:22, Galatians 1:8-9; *katara*: Galatians 3:10), he only uses *katara* with respect to Christ in keeping with Deuteronomy 21:23 in the LXX.

transubstantiation. The doctrine of transubstantiation maintains that the sacrifice of Christ continues in the regulated Mass:

> "The Holy Mass is the sacrifice of the body and blood of Jesus Christ, really present on the altar under the appearance of bread and wine, and offered to God for the living and the dead."[157]

To think that Christ is *continually* re-sacrificed is an outright denial of the fact that He *became a curse for us – once for all time.* Thus, the one who says that Jesus *is* accursed is not speaking from the Spirit's leading. Without a partitive analysis of such an utterance, some could be led astray. The Corinthians needed to learn how to scrutinize the words spoken in their assembly in order to judge the speaker, no matter what gift they claimed to possess.

Corinth's failures serve as a painful object lesson for those who refuse to apply the tests of love previously considered in Deuteronomy 13:1-5, 18-22, and Jeremiah 14:14-16. Especially deceptive were the false prophets who came to the people *in the name of the Lord (Yahweh),* giving the appearance of legitimacy to the unsuspecting:

> Jeremiah 14:14: "...The prophets are prophesying falsehood in My name. I have neither sent them nor commanded them nor spoken to them; they are prophesying to you a false vision, divination, futility and the deception of their own minds."

God's call for discernment in Jeremiah 14 strongly parallels Paul's instructions to the Corinthians. Those who claimed to deliver revelation by the Holy Spirit were to be evaluated in view what they said. These same Old Testament principles were applicable for the 1st century church

---

[157] Loraine Boettner, <u>Roman Catholicism</u>, (Phillipsburg/New Jersey: The Presbyterian and Reformed Publishing Company, 1962), 175.

as it was filled with the claimants of the apostolic and prophetic gifts. Even if one spoke in abundance of Christ and Him crucified as our penal substitute, the presence of the slightest error (even a verb tense) belied his claim. In the case of prophecy, their words will not contain *the deception of their own minds*, or as Peter said, "...no prophecy was ever made by an act of human will, but men moved by the Holy Spirit spoke from God" (2 Peter 1:21). Yet, Corinth continued to endure men who gave utterances, not by the Spirit, but by the machinations of their own minds; and this downgrade in their midst continued with devastating results. Despite their better beginning, Paul found himself exhorting a church that had tolerated immorality the likes of which did not exist among the Gentiles (1 Cor. 5:1); incorporated pagan practices and prostitution in their worship (1 Cor. 6:12-20); made dangerous flirtations with the pagan culture around them (1 Cor. 8 & 10); engaged in a bacchanalian degradation of the Lord's table (1 Cor. 11); and made theological flirtations with those who actually denied the resurrection (1 Cor. 15:12). Paul's painful pursuit for their progress continued, and after writing his "sorrowful" letter, Paul issued this warning in 2 Corinthians:

> **2 Corinthians 11:1–4:** 1 I wish that you would bear with me in a little foolishness; but indeed you are bearing with me. 2 For I am jealous for you with a godly jealousy; for I betrothed you to one husband, so that to Christ I might present you as a pure virgin. 3 But I am afraid that, as the serpent deceived Eve by his craftiness, your minds will be led astray from the simplicity and purity of devotion to Christ. 4 For if one comes and preaches another Jesus whom we have not preached, or you receive a different spirit which you have not received, or a different gospel which you have not accepted, you bear this beautifully.

The gravity of Paul's stated concern should not be underestimated. The deception that was taking place in Corinth was similar to that of Galatia. False Gospels were being accepted without a shred of critical analysis:

Galatians 1:6–9: 6 I am amazed that you are so quickly deserting Him who called you by the grace of Christ, for a different gospel; 7 which is really not another; only there are some who are disturbing you and want to distort the gospel of Christ. 8 But even if we, or an angel from heaven, should preach to you a gospel contrary to what we have preached to you, he is to be accursed! 9 As we have said before, so I say again now, if any man is preaching to you a gospel contrary to what you received, he is to be accursed!

Paul twice repeats the curse of God (*anathema*) upon the false messengers of an alternate gospel. The strength and force of his warning to the Galatians parallels his conclusion to 1 Corinthians 16:22 "If anyone does not love the Lord, he is to be accursed [*anathema*]..." It also parallels Paul's warning concerning those who appear as messengers of God:

2 Corinthians 11:13–15: 13 For such men are false apostles, deceitful workers, disguising themselves as apostles of Christ. 14 No wonder, for even Satan disguises himself as an angel of light. 15 Therefore it is not surprising if his servants also disguise themselves as servants of righteousness, whose end will be according to their deeds.

Paul's comparison of the Corinthians to Eve, who was deceived by the serpent in the garden, provides a striking parallel to Galatians 1:6-9. When we examine these warnings, side by side, we see that Paul was helping the churches to have a needed awareness of Satan's historic schemes. Satan's messengers do not announce themselves when they enter the church, instead they creep in unnoticed beneath the false guise of legitimacy.[158] This is why we see such a repeated stress on the church's responsibility to *test the spirits*, knowing that *false prophets* and *false teachers* abound in the world, secretly introducing their destructive heresies.[159] Clearly, Paul had a grave concern for heretical and demonic

---

[158] Jude 4.
[159] 1 John 4:1, 2 Peter 2:1.

influence in all the churches, especially at Galatia and Corinth in light of their spiritual downgrade. Remarkably, Grudem's loose interpretation of 1 Corinthians 14:5 & 29 undermines the church's call to discernment concerning those who claim to speak by the leading of the Holy Spirit. In the case of 1 Corinthians 14:5, Grudem even suggests that Paul was unconcerned about the danger of demonic influence amongst the Corinthians:

> "Paul says, 'I want you all to speak in tongues' (1 Cor. 14:5). He gives no warning that they should beware of demonic counterfeit or even think that this would be a possibility when they use this gift."[160]

Grudem's shocking oversimplification of Paul's teaching is alarming, the implications of which pose a great danger to the church. Any indifference to corruption poses a great danger to the church of any age, whether such corruption comes by means of demonic influence, false apostles, false prophets, false teachers, or all of these combined. Grudem seems to forget Paul's teaching to the Corinthians whereby he reminded them that Satan's messengers come disguised as the *servants of righteousness* such that their corruptions are well disguised. If Paul was so unconcerned about demonic influences in Corinth, then why did he mention such standards of evaluation to begin with? Why would he later write to the church, warning them about their deadly liaisons with Satan's messengers in their midst (2 Corinthians 11:1-15)? To suggest that Paul was unconcerned about demonic influence within the Corinthian church is simply incredible. Though Grudem's above citation of 1 Corinthians 14:5 is employed in order to emphasize the use of tongues only, the context of this passage is about the *supremacy of prophecy over tongues*. When we consider Grudem's teaching up to this point, two matters of concern come to mind: 1. What Grudem says in this passage reminds us, once

---

[160] Grudem, Systematic Theology, 1077 (E.2.h. What About the Danger of Demonic Counterfeit?).

again, of his strong deference for the argument of ignorance. Paul doesn't say many things in 1 Corinthians 14:5, but this should not lead us to conclude that he was indifferent to whatever Grudem imagines is missing in the text; 2. His translation of the word *thelō* as *"want"* rather than *"wish"* makes Paul sound as if he is delivering an *exhortative injunction*, rather than offering a *hypothetical musing*, thus, Grudem is willing to press his nuanced interpretation of just one word to such an extent that he actually concludes that Paul was unconcerned about the spread of counterfeit gifts and demonic influence within the Corinthian church (*via* tongues or otherwise), despite the overwhelming evidence to the contrary. Despite this, Grudem presses his point rather consistently:

> "If Paul was eager for the gift of prophecy to function at Corinth, troubled as the church was by immaturity, selfishness, divisions, and other problems, then should we not also actively seek this valuable gift in our congregations today?...might a greater openness to the gift of prophecy perhaps help to correct a dangerous imbalance in church life, an imbalance that comes because we are too exclusively intellectual, objective, and narrowly doctrinal?"[161]

Grudem's assumption that Paul wanted all to prophecy (1 Corinthians 14:5) leads him to conclude that personal maturity is irrelevant in the pursuit and exercise of such a gift. His argument essentially suggests that if Paul wanted *all the Corinthians* to prophecy, including those who heralded insufferable standards of immorality, sin, compromise, and false doctrine, then such a low standard should be applied in the promotion of *fallible prophecy* in the modern day. By pressing this nuanced interpretation of his, Grudem has effectively gutted the heart of Paul's argument in all of 1 Corinthians, especially chapter 13. For Paul, the foundation of all Christian conduct was the fruit of the Spirit, *beginning with love*:

---

[161] Ibid., 1060.

Galatians 5:22–23: 22 But the fruit of the Spirit is love, joy, peace, patience, kindness, goodness, faithfulness, 23 gentleness, self-control; against such things there is no law.

Paul's principal mention of love in this passage is consistent with his instructions elsewhere on the true nature of love. Love is *first* in the list because it is the cornerstone of all the other qualities mentioned. In fact, a careful perusal of 1 Corinthians 13 reveals a strong parallel of thought to Galatians 5:22-23: "love is patient, love is kind and is not jealous; love does not brag and is not arrogant, does not act unbecomingly; it does not seek its own, is not provoked, does not take into account a wrong suffered, does not rejoice in unrighteousness, but rejoices in the truth; bears all things, believes all things, hopes all things, endures all things" (1 Corinthians 13:4-7). This principal fruit of the Spirit (love) is the very bedrock upon which Paul said, "if I have the gift of prophecy, and know all mysteries, and all knowledge; and if I have all faith, so as to remove mountains, but do not have love, I am nothing" (1 Corinthians 13:2). For Paul, maturity in the Spirit was everything, but for Grudem, *immaturity* supplies no hindrance to the pursuit of *fallible prophecy*. Thus, Grudem's argument that immaturity should not be seen as a barrier to the exercise of the gift of prophecy is nothing less than a bold and dangerous refutation of Paul's core instructions and warnings to the church at Corinth and, by extension, to the church in the present day.

Grudem's belief that New Testament prophecy was common, not being inhibited by corruption or severe immaturity (1 Corinthians 14:5) is utterly unsupported by the scriptural data. As well, his position that the claimants of prophecy were to be accepted by the church despite their erroneous utterances (1 Corinthians 14:29) is equally unsubstantiated. As to this latter defense of *fallible prophecy*, Grudem also utilizes 1 Thessalonians 5:21 for his position:

1 Thessalonians 5:20–21: 20 do not despise prophetic utterances. 21 But examine everything carefully; hold fast to that which is good;

Similar to his use of 1 Corinthians 14:29, Grudem argues that Paul's instruction to the Thessalonians affirms the presence of *fallible prophecy*: "'hold fast what is good,' implies that some of what is tested will not be good."[162] Grudem is right to assume that the implied message of verse 21 is that *some of what is tested will not be good*, but he is wrong to presume a response of *unqualified acceptance of the erroneous messenger*. Compton has well refuted Grudem's assumptions about this passage:

> "...Grudem points to 1 Thessalonians 5:20–21, 'Do not despise prophetic utterances, but examine everything carefully,' as the key parallel in support of his interpretation of 1 Corinthians 14:29. Yet the verb used in 1 Thessalonians 5:21 is the same verb used in 1 John 4:1 where John says, 'Test the spirits to see whether they are from God, because many false prophets have gone out into the world.' Clearly in 1 John 4:1 the verb has the idea of testing the prophets to judge the true from the false, as even Grudem acknowledges."[163]

One of the core dangers of *fallible prophecy* is the manner in which it subverts the ancient standards of testing and discerning false prophets. The redaction and removal of these tests poses a grave danger to the church, leaving brethren with the false belief that *genuine prophets speak an admixture of truth and error*. Grudem's failure to examine the parallel text of 1 John 4:1 is not surprising. Moreover, his use of 1 Thessalonians 5:21 is problematically and consistently detached from the very next verse in the instruction set: "...hold fast to that which is good; *abstain from every form of evil*" (1 Thessalonians 5:21b-22, italics mine). This contrast of thought is essential for us to understand the whole of Paul's developed thought. The binary nature of Paul's instruction is fairly simple and it reflects the same instructions found in the Old Testament concerning the

---

[162] Grudem, The Gift of Prophecy, 367.
[163] Compton, The Continuation of New Testament Prophecy, 8.

tests for prophecy. As we learned in *Chapter 1: Prophecy – A Test of Love*, when the claimant of prophecy was found to be false, the prophet was declared to be "evil" (H. *ra'*, G. *ponēron*) such that he was to be purged from Israel's assembly: *"that prophet shall die" (Deut. 18:20)* and *"So you shall purge the evil from among you" (Deut. 13:5)*.[164] This familiar injunction, *"you shall purge the evil from among you,"* which is repeated ten times in Deuteronomy, consistently referred to the death of the one deemed as *evil*. In the Septuagint, the word used for *evil* is *ponēros* which is the same term that Paul used in 1 Thessalonians 5:22 and 1 Corinthians 5:21 (*"...remove the wicked man from among yourselves."*). As we already discussed, the new order of the New Covenant calls for *church discipline* rather than the death of the offender. Such was the case for Paul's dealings with the Corinthian church, and such is the case for his instructions to the Thessalonians. Paul's antithesis between good and evil in 1 Thessalonians 5:21-22 is quite strong and clear: "...hold fast to that which is good, abstain from every form of evil [*ponērou*]." We should also note that Paul's injunction is devoid of any exceptions: "abstain from *every form [pantos eidous]* of evil." The Greek word for *form [eidous]* speaks of the form of things based upon sight or observation. Thus, this term speaks of the form or substance of things based upon empirical analysis of that which is observed.[165] Thus, Paul's command to abstain from such *evil* is rooted in this matter of observation and analysis. Such observation and analysis we have already seen prescribed in texts such as Deuteronomy 13:1-5, 18:18-22; Jeremiah 14:14-16; Matthew 7:15-23, 24:24; Corinthians 12:3, 13, 14:29, 16:22; and Galatians 5:2-23. False prophesy encompasses multiple forms of evil, and all of it must be rejected: prophesies issued in the name of false gods; prophesies falsely issued in the name of the true God; prophesies issued by prideful

---

[164] References to death: Deut. 13:6; 17:7, 12; 19:13; 21:21, 22, 24; 24:7. The one possible exception is Deuteronomy 19:19, which could apply to a lesser sentence than death in some cases (v. 21).

[165] Luke 3:22, 9:29; John 5:37.

presumption, fleshliness, malicious intent, and lovelessness – all such *forms* of false prophecy, and the false prophets who deliver them, are to be classified as evil and resisted as such. Alternately, valid prophecies and the prophets who deliver them are to be embraced as *good.*

Any form of compromise from these prophetic tests is not only dangerous, it is unloving.[166]

In all of this, we must recognize that the notion of a third category of prophecy (*fallible prophecy*) is nothing less than a human contrivance. Scripture presents only two categories of prophecy: *prophētēs* (prophet) and *pseudoprophētēs* (false prophet). Out of this reality, Christ warned the disciples concerning the manner in which false prophets present themselves:

Matthew 7:15–23: 15 "Beware of the false prophets (*pseudoprophētai*), who come to you in sheep's clothing, but inwardly are ravenous wolves. 16 "You will know them by their fruits. Grapes are not gathered from thorn bushes nor figs from thistles, are they? 17 "So every good tree bears good fruit, but the bad tree bears bad fruit. 18 "A good tree cannot produce bad fruit, nor can a bad tree produce good fruit. 19 "Every tree that does not bear good fruit is cut down and thrown into the fire. 20 "So then, you will know them by their fruits. 21 "Not everyone who says to Me, 'Lord, Lord,' will enter the kingdom of heaven, but he who does the will of My Father who is in heaven will enter. 22 "Many will say to Me on that day, 'Lord, Lord, did we not prophesy in Your name, and in Your name cast out demons, and in Your name perform many miracles?' 23 "And then I will declare to them, 'I never knew you; DEPART FROM ME, YOU WHO PRACTICE LAWLESSNESS.'

Pseudo (false) prophets come cloaked with the garb of legitimacy and truth. Armed with an abundance of *words* and *works*, they are adorned with a religious appearance which covers their inner corruption and,

---

[166] Deuteronomy 13:1-5.

sadly, some are *self-deceived*. In view of this, Christ's warning is both serious and needful. Yet we might wonder how the disciples should have deciphered the Savior's teaching if *fallible prophecy* were actually true. Would the disciples have understood Christ's instructions and warnings beneath the pretense of a third category of prophecy: *fallible prophecy?* If so, how were they to apply Jesus' teaching? Were the disciples to accept all claimants of the prophetic gift even if their lives were corrupted with sin and immaturity, or their utterances were fraught with error? Were they to receive the testimony of such "prophets" in view of their willingness to confess Jesus as their Lord, especially in view of Grudem's teaching?:

> "...we can distinguish true from false prophecy on the basis of willingness to acknowledge Jesus Christ as Lord (1 Cor. 12:3)."[167]

Grudem's standard clearly falls short of the Savior's teaching: "Many will say to Me on that day, 'Lord, Lord, did we not prophesy in Your name...'" (Matthew 7:22), as well as Paul's who indicated that a man may confess the Lordship of Christ but "if anyone does not love the Lord, he is to be accursed" (1 Corinthians 16:22). In the end, all forms of evil in association with false prophecy (utterances, actions, and motives) must be refused by the body of Christ. Yet, with the infusion of *fallible prophecy*, such principles and prescriptions become confused, corrupted, and even eliminated.

In the end, the binary reality of *true and false prophets* underscored the teachings and warnings issued to the New Testament Church. Paul's

---

[167] Grudem, The Gift of Prophecy, 289. Grudem's contention that "...we can distinguish true from false prophecy on the basis of willingness to acknowledge Jesus Christ as Lord (1 Cor. 12:3)" is simply untenable. In light of Paul's emphasis on love (1 Corinthians 13) and his warnings about the disguised messengers of Satan (2 Corinthians 11), it seems difficult to imagine that Paul believed that the claimants of revelation were to be known by their words *alone*.

warnings to the Corinthians were remarkably similar to those given to the church at Galatia. Both churches needed to understand that the false messengers of Satan enter into the church beneath the guise of sheep's clothing. In the case of the Corinthians, Satan's messengers entered in with talk about the resurrection, the penal sacrifice of Christ, the church, salvation, grace, and the worship of God; but their words and their deeds revealed their true nature. In the case of Galatia, the Judaizers spoke, in abundance, of Christ, his sacrifice, good works, and the authority of Scripture. To the unsuspecting, this placed them well within the camp of Christianity. Yet, these false messengers added the works of the Law to their version of the Gospel – thereby nullifying their message altogether. If the church is going to be the pillar and support of truth,[168] then divine revelation must be sought out as the only sure foundation.[169] Satan's methods have never really changed. From his incremental obfuscations of God's commands in the garden, to his disguised deceptions of the present day, Satan is seeking ways to present his messengers as servants of righteousness though they are the messengers of death. Of course, their message is a blended one – containing a veneer of truth with just enough error to transform the true Gospel into that which is worthy of the anathema of God. Therefore, it doesn't matter who the messenger of Satan is: a professed apostle, prophet, speaker/interpreter of tongues, pastor, teacher, or an angel of light – all must be scrutinized by that which has been supernaturally revealed by the true God. Nevertheless, it is especially important to adjudicate those who claim to possess those unique gifts which, by ancient *scriptural definitions*, lay claim to *infallible divine revelation from God: apostles and prophets*. This is so for one simple reason: unlike a pastor or teacher who can and will misspeak on occasion,[170] just a *single error* from an apostle or prophet belies the very nature of their *professed* office; and such error amounts to blasphemy

---

[168] 1 Timothy 3:15.
[169] Ephesians 2:20.
[170] James 3:1-2.

against the true God *who never misspeaks.* Ultimately, toleration of such blasphemy is unloving (Deuteronomy 13:1-5, 1 Corinthians 13, 16:22) since it heralds the desires of men above the truth of God.

The ancient standard of scrutiny for any messenger claiming to be a spokesman for God remains as an integral part of the church's pursuit of purity and maturation – and overall – *it remains as a central test and evidence of genuine love for the Lord.*

CONCLUSION:

THE FALLIBLE PROPHETS OF

NEW CALVINISM

In this final chapter, it will be our task to draw from our previous studies and consider the potential impact that *fallible prophecy* will have on the church, both now and in the future. We will also consider the means by which *fallible prophecy* is being promoted and encouraged in the present day. All of this is designed to help us comprehend why such a subject is worthy of our attention *and response.* There are many theological movements that come and go; some that make strong inroads into the church, and others that die out rather quickly. In the case of *fallible prophecy,* we have yet to see what the future will hold for this doctrine and its influence on the church, but it is this author's contention that *fallible prophecy* poses a great risk to the body of Christ. Should the church fail to examine this doctrine carefully, she may continue to fall prey to its increasing influence.

Some may suggest at this point that *fallible prophecy* is a harmless concept and that it hasn't the potential for any real harm in the body of Christ, yet I would suggest that this is dangerous thinking. In review of what has been previously examined, consider the following:

- By changing and redacting the scriptural concept of prophecy, the advocates of *fallible prophecy* have created a host of doctrinal problems and points of confusion within the church. God's promise is clear: "So will My word be which goes forth from My mouth; It will not return to Me empty, without accomplishing what I desire" (Isaiah 55:11), yet in *fallible prophecy,* such a promise is negated by human corruption. Thus, *fallible prophecy* not only transforms core constructs of *ecclesiology,* but it also raises fundamental questions about *theology proper,* that is, *what can be said about a deity that tries, ineffectually, to communicate through prophetic intermediaries?*

- In light of its problematic interpretations of prophecy, *fallible prophecy* promotes subjectivism among Christians and supplies a dangerous form of protection for *false prophets,* whether they are self-deceived or intentional deceivers of others.

- The consciences of believers can be unnecessarily bound by supposed prophecies that cannot be fully and objectively evaluated. Christians who obey or resist such "prophecies" cannot fully know if they are obeying or disobeying God's directives due to the presence of human *fallibility and error.*

- We examined the most central and explicit example of a New Testament prophet: Agabus. If the advocates of *fallible prophecy* applied his example consistently, in view of their own interpretations, then no prophecy would ever need to be obeyed in view of the presence of human error. By the central example of Agabus, one must wonder why such "prophecy" should be sought out by the church at all.

- The doctrine of *fallible prophecy* posits the view that *nearly everyone* within the local church can have and exercise the gift of prophecy, leading to the false presumption that severe spiritual immaturity poses no barrier to the exercise of such a gift. Yet, such a conclusion as this is a direct contradiction to Paul's central emphasis on love in 1 Corinthians 13.

- In the New Testament we see repeated lessons on the supremacy of the New Covenant over the Old, yet how does a degraded form of prophecy (*fallible* New Testament prophecy) demonstrate such supremacy of the New Covenant in Christ's blood?

In addition to the above, the advocates of *fallible prophecy* argue that the presence of such prophecy in the local church is a sign of God's blessing, while its absence is a sign of God's removal of favor from His people.[171] They maintain this view while simultaneously arguing that *fallible prophecy* has less authority than the teaching of the Scriptures.[172] Though it may not be intended, such a view gravely diminishes non-continuationist churches, even if such churches hold a very high view of

---

[171] Grudem, The Gift of Prophecy, 282.
[172] Grudem, Systematic Theology, 1058.

the teaching/preaching of the Word. It should be no surprise, therefore, that *fallible prophecy* enthusiasts seek to promote and spread their doctrine to others. In his *Systematic Theology*, Wayne Grudem supplies a 6-step process for introducing *fallible prophecy* to the local church. Within Grudem's 6-point plan, he advises his readers to seek out permission from their church's leadership to advance such a ministry. In light of this, one must wonder: if *fallible prophecy* were true, being the sovereign provision of the Spirit, then why would it be necessary to seek permission from the leadership of a local church in such a matter – especially if nearly all can exercise such a gift? If *fallible prophecy* is such a bedrock ministry of any true church, then should we not expect this gift to spread without restraint, with or without the permission of mere men? Yet, despite these questions and inconsistencies, *fallible prophecy* continues to advance in the modern day, particularly by means of the *New Calvinism* movement. New Calvinism, which is supported by a growing number of continuationist teachers with Reformed leanings, continues to increase dramatically. Citing Time Magazine's March 2009 article, *The New Calvinism*,[173] popular pastor and author Mark Driscoll called New Calvinism "...the third biggest idea that is changing the world right now," praising it for its continuationist influence upon the modern church:

"Old Calvinism was cessationistic and fearful of the presence and power of the Holy Spirit. New Calvinism is continuationist and joyful in the presence and power of the Holy Spirit."[174]

---

[173] David Van Biema, The New Calvinism, (Time Magazine, March 12th 2009), http://content.time.com/time/specials/packages/article/0,28804,1884779_1884782_18847 60,00.html.

[174] Mark Driscoll, Time Magazine Names New Calvinism 3rd Most Powerful Idea, (Resurgence Website, March 12 2009). http://theresurgence.com/2009/03/12/time-magazine-names-new-calvinism-3rd-most-powerful-idea.

Driscoll's views are revealing. His comments remind us that continuationist thinking has served as a Trojan horse through which *fallible prophecy* continually infiltrates the Reformed community. By this comparison of his,[175] Driscoll exposes a dangerous over-confidence alongside his reckless disregard for historic Calvinism:

"At its heart, Reformed and Puritan theology is pietistic; the concern of Reformation theology is as practical as it is doctrinal. As the majority of the orthodox divines affirm, theology is partly theoretical, partly practical (*partim partim*); the head and heart are necessary corollaries of each other. For Calvin and the Puritans, reformation of the church involved the reform of piety, or spirituality, as much as a reform of theology…this dual emphasis of nurturing the mind and the soul is sorely needed today. On one hand, we confront the problem of dry, Reformed orthodoxy, which correctly teaches doctrine but lacks emphasis on vibrant, godly living. The result is that people bow before the doctrine of God without yearning for a vital, spiritual union with the God of doctrine. On the other hand, Pentecostal and charismatic Christians propose emotionalism in protesting a formal, lifeless Christianity, but this

---

[175] Mark Driscoll recently summarized a comparison of the "New Calvinist" movement to that of the Puritans of yesteryear: "Old Calvinism was fundamental or liberal and separated from or syncretized with culture. New Calvinism is missional and seeks to create and redeem culture. Old Calvinism fled from the cities. New Calvinism is flooding into cities. Old Calvinism was cessationistic and fearful of the presence and power of the Holy Spirit. New Calvinism is continuationist and joyful in the presence and power of the Holy Spirit. Old Calvinism was fearful and suspicious of other Christians and burned bridges. New Calvinism loves all Christians and builds bridges between them." Driscoll's comparison is deeply flawed. Anyone who has studied the Puritans and Reformers of yesteryear would know better than to say that such saints were "fearful of the presence and power of the Holy Spirit" as if to say that they were not "joyful in the presence and power of the Holy Spirit." Driscoll's capacity to miss the mark concerning church history is breathtaking and reveals a certain naiveté of some within the "Emergent" and "New Calvinist" movements. I should here note that the object of this article is not to defend the theological system of "Calvinism" *per se*. Though I prefer not to *identify* myself with the label "Calvinist, I do strongly align myself with the Puritans of yesteryear in light of their Evangelical commitment to a sound theology, soteriology, harmartiology, anthropology, missiology, and Christology.

emotionalism is not solidly rooted in Scripture. The result is that people put human feeling above the triune God as He reveals Himself in Scripture. The genius of genuine reformed piety is that it marries theology and piety so that head, heart, and hand motivate one another to live for God's glory and our neighbor's well-being."[176]

Driscoll's assertion that "Old Calvinism" was fearful of the presence and power of the Holy Spirit is simply off the mark. Multiple aspects of New Calvinism are indeed *new*, but this is not entirely a compliment. Moreover, *fallible prophecy* is indeed new, but it offers no scriptural improvement or benefit to the body of Christ. Despite this, *fallible prophecy* continues to receive significant support from its advocates. We have already mentioned the influences of Wayne Grudem and D.A. Carson, but must also mention John Piper who is considered to be a father figure to the New Calvinism movement.[177] John Piper's support for the teachings of Wayne Grudem has been evident for many years, however, he recently articulated his defense of *fallible prophecy* in an interview with David Matthis *via* his *Desiring God* Ministry:

David Mathis: "John there's a difference on the surface of how prophecy seems to function – the Old Covenant and the New Covenant; the Old Covenant 'Thus Saith the Lord' and there's a different sense in the way prophecy seems to function in the New Covenant. How have you put that together in your thinking and during your practical ministry?"

---

[176] Joel R. Beeke & Mark Jones, <u>A Puritan Theology: *Doctrine for Life*</u>, (Grand Rapids MI: Reformation Heritage Books), 849.

[177] "John Piper is the father figure of the 'Neo-Calvinist' movement that includes younger ministers like Mark Driscoll, Joshua Harris and many of the writers at the Gospel Coalition site." Rev. Jonathan Weyer, <u>Rob Bell vs. John Piper: Do We Have to Choose?</u>, (Huffington Post Religion Page):
http://www.huffingtonpost.com/rev-jonathan-weyer/rob-bell-vs-john-piper-do_b_829956.html.

Piper: "It's not just a surface difference, there's a substantial difference. It is remarkable that the Apostles are not called prophets. This new office seen to be brought in by Jesus of Apostle instead of saying I'm going to gather around me an Isaiah, and an Ezekial, and a Daniel, I'm gonna gather a Paul, a Peter, and a John and call them Apostles. And, I've been significantly influenced by Wayne Grudem's book on prophecy, trying to make sense out of texts like 1 Thessalonians 5 – "test all things, hold fast to what is good... don't despise prophecies." That's been really relevant in my own personal experience because I think our tendency is to despise what the New Testament treats as prophecy. Um, prophecy in the NT, at least the way it's treated in 1 Corinthians 12, 13, 14, doesn't appear to have the same Scripture quality, inerrant inspiration and authority that when an Isaiah – 'thus saith the Lord' – you don't go up to Isaiah and say 'I'm gonna test what you said and hold fast to what is good and throw the rest away.' But you do that with NT prophecy. You test it and if it proves good, that is conforming to the authoritative teaching of the Apostles, then you embrace it. And so, prophecy in the NT seems to be down a notch from the authority of OT prophets and is to be exposed to testing which is based upon the apostolic teaching which would have the prophecy level quality of the authority of the OT and then it would be God bringing something to mind, which is pretty much the language that Wayne Grudem uses, God bringing something to mind that you otherwise would not have thought of..."[178]

Within the interview, Piper mentions one of his experiences with *fallible prophecy* in response to another question by David Mathis

David Mathis: "For a non-preacher who has an impression, they think from God, to help somebody – consolation, encouragement for them – any counsel for how to go about communicating that?"

John Piper: "When I was trying to help our people with these things years ago and teach them to be open to the Spirit and pursuing the Spirit – not just

---

[178] David Matthis, Piper on Prophecy and Tongues, (desiringGod Blog, January 17th 2013) http://www.desiringgod.org/blog/posts/piper-on-prophecy-and-tongues

cautiously open you know like some people say – but the Bible says earnestly desire spiritual gifts, especially that you may prophecy; and so I'm encouraging our people to seek the spiritual gifts so that we can minister graces to each other, love, joy, peace, patience, goodness, kindness; those and the gifts, you know, the gift faith and the gift of miracles and the gift of healing and the gift of tongues and the gift of teaching and interpretation and all those things – go ahead, ask the Lord for those things – don't make him give you anything, but just ask Him. Well, a woman came to me while my wife is pregnant with my fourth child and she says: 'I have a very hard prophecy for you' I said OK – she said... in fact she wrote it down and gave it to me – 'Your wife is gonna die in childbirth, and you're gonna have a daughter.' I went back to my study - I thanked her, I said 'I appreciate that' – I forget what I said, but it wasn't...I didn't want to hear that. I went back to my study, I got down and I just wept. I said, 'Lord I have been trying to help these people take this gift seriously and I don't know what to do with this. This is...I cannot imagine why this would be helpful. It doesn't feel like it's of You, and yet I don't want to discourage people.' So I kept it totally to myself. I didn't tell Noel my wife about it and when we delivered our fourth boy, not girl, I gave a 'whoop' which I always do, but this 'whoop' was a little extra because I knew as soon as the boy was born this was not a true prophecy and Noel is still alive and Barnabas is, what, 27 years old today; but that's the sort of thing that makes you despise prophecy – you just say 'I don't want anything to do with that kind of stuff' and I don't blame people for feeling that way but the Bible says, don't despise them; be careful and discerning and so, my answer to your question is: if you sense something you have for somebody, offer it them as a gift, don't thrust it at them as a demand – 'I sense' - I would use the words like, 'I sense that God wants me to say to you.' ...Offer gifts to people – these are spiritual gifts, these are not spiritual hammers. And so, offer it to them and say, 'just test it and if it seems to help, wonderful.'"[179]

Piper's example is interesting and raises further questions about the application of *fallible prophecy*. Before delving into his example I must mention that Piper's expressed relief after the safe delivery of his fourth

---

[179] Ibid.

boy is perfectly understandable *in the most immediate sense.* The prospect of losing his wife during childbirth would have been gripping – it would be gripping for anyone. Yet, what is to be learned from his example?:

- Piper's initial response after the birth of his son was to give a celebratory "whoop," saying "I knew as soon as the boy was born this was not a true prophecy." Though we can understand his celebratory spirit over the safety of his wife, what should one think or say about the presence of false prophecy in the local church? Does genuine prophecy have at its center one's subjective desires for the future?

- Though Piper recounts the story from the standpoint of hindsight, we should wonder how he could have known that this was a false prophecy from the beginning, as he said: "I cannot imagine why this would be helpful. It doesn't feel like it's of You..." In what sense might this not have *felt* to be of the Lord and by what scriptural standard did he make such an initial assessment? Apart from any scriptural test, is the criterion for testing a *fallible prophecy* to be reduced to the subjective question of one's own "feelings?"

- Based upon Piper's own counsel, would his encounter with the unnamed woman have been improved at all had she prefaced her "hard prophecy" with: "I sense that God wants me to say this to you," concluding her utterance by saying "I offer this as a gift."?

- In Piper's cited example, no single aspect of this woman's "prophecy" was valid, except for the mention of *pregnancy* – a fact that would have been visibly evident to all. Piper correctly calls the prophecy "false," however, we hear nothing in his testimony about the scripturally requisite tests of love being applied to this situation (Deuteronomy 13:1-5, 1 Corinthians 13). With the presence of a false prophet in the church, such tests are not an option. Perhaps there was a follow-up provided to this situation, but if this is the case, we are left without the central lesson of such a follow-up. Thus, one must wonder if this woman is still in the church today practicing her "gift," thereby binding the consciences of others with her falsely claimed prophecies; or has she moved on to other churches unabatedly spreading her influence to others?

Piper's example raises questions about what it takes for a *fallible prophet* to merit the correct identity of a *false prophet*. How much more error or presumption is needed in order for a church to recognize that such claims to prophecy are indeed false? If the Lord is truly testing His people in view of the prescribed tests of prophecy, then how does the infusion of *fallible prophecy,* along with its enshrined error, aid in such a process; and in what sense does any of this communicate the supremacy of the New Covenant over that of the Old? With *fallible prophecy,* error is a protected reality within the "gift." Because of this, the historic meaning of prophecy is utterly turned on its head while prophetic errorists freely wander about in the church. Addressing the need for judging the claimants of prophecy, Ian Hamilton said the following in his debate with Wayne Grudem at the Proclamation Trust debate on prophecy:

Ian Hamilton: "I think that it's more likely that Paul is saying [in 1 Corinthians 14:29] that the others, either the other prophets or as you would argue, I think, the congregation as a whole had to judge in this very fertile congregation at Corinth where error and truth were being mixed all the time with false prophets, super apostles were coming in; that Paul was saying: 'you need to learn to judge between men who are true prophets and who are false prophets.' And I think that stands very well with 1 John 4:1, 'test the spirits'; with our Lord Jesus Christ's warning to the church in Matthew 7 of false prophets: men in sheep's clothing; but even if it didn't mean not discriminate among men, but discriminate the content of what they are saying, would that not simply be all at peace with Deuteronomy 13, Deuteronomy 18 and the whole concern that the people of God, because of satanic activity, were always being infected with surreptitious false teachers who needed to be exposed?"

Wayne Grudem: "I don't see in the NT any parallel to the treatment of prophets in the OT where they were taken out and stoned or the NT equivalent would be excommunication; it's rather Paul saying, 'don't despise prophecies, hold fast to what is good.' So, false teachers are certainly condemned and should be excluded, but not anybody who makes a mistake on a prophecy."[180]

By Grudem's own standard, no one who *makes a mistake on a prophecy* should face the corrective measures of church discipline. It should be evident that the advocates of *fallible prophecy* have enshrined *error* within their concept of biblical prophecy and that such error should never be seen as evidence of a false prophet. By this standard *of his*, the scriptural tests of love become buried in the ash heap of the contrivance of *fallible prophecy*. The danger of operating by one's own subjective impression is not at all new. The church has had to battle with this matter for centuries, and this battle continues in the present day as Hamilton notes:

"I find the view that Wayne espouses, pastorally, um...let me choose my words carefully, at best they could cause tremendous confusion in a church. A prophet stands up and says, 'I'm fairly certain...' and those are the two words that Wayne uses in his doctoral thesis, '...I'm fairly certain God is saying '[Mary] is to marry Phillip.' I think I would want to stand and say, 'well are you sure it's Phillip? Maybe it's John.' And, 'are you sure it's Mary? Maybe it's Margaret.' 'Fairly Certain' never seems to describe the prophetic utterances both of the Old Covenant Scriptures and the New Covenant Scriptures; when prophets spoke they said, 'Thus saith the Lord.' And if we have men or women standing up in congregations saying that they think they might have a word from the Lord, that is binding the conscience of individual Christians beyond that which the infallible Holy Scriptures would suggest to us and give to us."[181]

Hamilton touches on a crucial point of concern. Whatever nomenclature one wishes to use - "I *sense* that God wants me to say; I am *fairly certain* that God has said; I offer this as a *gift*," -any such "prophecy" places the

---

[180] Wayne Grudem and Ian Hamilton, Debate chaired by Adrian Reynolds, <u>Not by Might nor by Power</u>, (The Proclamation Trust, 2010):
https://vimeo.com/37169587.
[181] Ibid.

recipient in the challenging position of having to wonder *if in fact* God is *attempting* to deliver a direct revelation. The ineffectual nature of *fallible prophecy* is disconcerting enough by itself. What exactly can be said about a deity that merely *attempts* to communicate with men and is often thwarted by the fallibility of human instruments? In addition to this, such fallible utterances produce an abundance of uncertainty in the mind of the recipient. In such a situation, relevant questions should come flooding into the conscience of believers as they attempt to sift and sort through any supposed "prophecy." Questions about the potential for truth or error in the "prophecy" would dominate their thinking in addition to a host of subjective considerations about whether or not the utterance "feels" like it is from the Lord. Unlike the clarity of genuine prophecy, *fallible prophecy* has the massive potential of binding the believer with the needless yoke of fear, doubt, and uncertainty. Since *fallible prophecies* are resistible, those who choose to reject such utterances are left to wonder if in fact they are guilty of resisting a genuine word from the Lord. Alternately, those who obey such utterances must wonder whether or not they are obeying the machinations of men as opposed to God's actual revelation. Scripture does no such thing, but *fallible prophecy does.* John Owen rightly warns his readers, and us, of the dangers of those who *pretend falsely unto the inspiration of the Holy Spirit:*

> "...it is very probable, that when men falsely and in mere pretence took upon them to be prophets divinely inspired, without any antecedent diabolical enthusiasm, that the devil made use of them to compass his own designs. Being given up by the righteous judgment of God unto all delusions, for belying his spirit and holy inspirations, they were quickly possessed with a spirit of lying and unclean divination. So the false prophets of Ahab, who encouraged him to go up unto Ramoth Gilead, foretelling his prosperous success, 1 Kings xxii. 6. seemed only to have complied deceitfully with the inclinations of their master, and to have out-acted his other courtiers in flattery, by gilding it with a pretence of prophecy. But when Micaiah came to lay open the mystery of their iniquity, it appeared that a lying spirit by the permission of God had possessed

their minds, and gave them impressions, which being supernatural, they were deceived as well as they did deceive, ver. 21-23. This they were justly given up unto, pretending falsely unto the inspiration of that Holy Spirit, which they had not received. And no other-wise hath it fallen out with some in our days, whom we have seen visibly acted by an extraordinary power; unduly pretending unto supernatural agitations from God, they were really acted by the devil, a thing they neither desired nor looked after; but being surprised by it were pleased with it for a while; as it was with sundry of the Quakers at their first appearance."[182]

Any act of degrading, maligning, or falsifying the Spirit's work is a grave matter. It is therefore crucial that believers understand and appreciate the Spirit's leading as He bears fruit and supplies insight, illumination, and wisdom through the Scriptures. However, those who insist on equating this work of the Spirit with the unique gift of prophecy are engaging in a dangerous conflation. Ultimately, the church has all that she needs through the Spirit's illuminating work, whereby He equips God's people with the requisite wisdom needed to supply encouragement and admonishment within the body of Christ.[183] God's prophetic word, delivered once for all the saints, is living and active supplying such illumination, admonishment, encouragement, and conviction to the people of God:

Psalm 119:105: Your word is a lamp to my feet And a light to my path.

Hebrews 4:12: 12 For the word of God is living and active and sharper than any two-edged sword, and piercing as far as the division of soul and spirit, of both joints and marrow, and able to judge the thoughts and intentions of the heart.

---

[182] Owen, The Works of John Owen, 3:29-30.

[183] Romans 15:13–14: 13 Now may the God of hope fill you with all joy and peace in believing, so that you will abound in hope by the power of the Holy Spirit. 14 And concerning you, my brethren, I myself also am convinced that you yourselves are full of goodness, filled with all knowledge and able also to admonish one another.

Cessationists and Continuationists might agree on the authority of Scripture at some level, yet there is a crucial disparity between them concerning the Spirit-breathed[184] Scripture's *sole sufficiency* in the life of a believer. In the aforementioned 2010 Proclamation Trust debate, Grudem clarified such a position as follows:

"I understand that cessationists believe that the canon is closed, and I agree with that, but the question is not that of the canon; the question is: what about communication from God to specific individuals that is not part of the canon? If the Bible is the book of the covenant that stipulates the terms of the relationship between God as King and us as His covenant people, then are we to say that the King can never communicate with His people in any additional ways besides the covenant document? Can He who created speech and loves His people never speak to them directly and personally? The Cessationist position, if I understand it correctly, allows for no element of individual personal guidance from the Holy Spirit in the life of a Christian, ever, our guidance is simply to be taken from reading the Bible and using mature wisdom to apply it to our lives."[185]

Grudem's representation of the Cessationist position fails to recognize the conjoined reality of the word *and the Spirit* in the matter of illumination. The position of Cessationism is not that the word is sufficient by itself, but that the *word and the Spirit* is what is sufficient in the life of the genuine believer. In the end, there is no reasonable sense in which the Holy Spirit can be separated from Holy Writ, or as Paul calls it: the sword of the Spirit which is the word of God (Ephesians 6:17). What is profoundly different between cessationists and continuationists is that the latter group insists on utilizing the label of *prophecy* for some things that a cessationist would call *illumination,* insisting that God continues to

---

[184] 2 Timothy 3:16.
[185] Grudem and Hamilton, <u>Not by Might nor by Power,</u>
https://vimeo.com/37169587.

supply *direct revelation* to His people. By insisting on the need for *new and direct revelation (immediate inspiration)*, the continuationist resultantly diminishes the Spirit's crucial ministry of illumining the Scriptures within the hearts and minds of God's people. Such illumination of the Scriptures has supplied God's people with a necessary standard by which all matters of life and doctrine can and must be measured. Charles Hodge unveils this historic challenge within the early church when he said:

"(1 Corinthians 14:37) Nobody had a right to consider himself inspired or to demand that others regard him in this way who did not conform to the instructions of men whose inspiration was beyond doubt. Thus, too, the apostle John commands Christians, 'Do not believe every spirit, but test the spirits to see whether they are from God, because many false prophets have gone out into the world' (1 John 4:1). And in verse 6 he gives the standard by which these prophets were to be tried: 'We are from God, and whoever knows God listens to us; but whoever is not from God does not listen to us. This is how we recognize the Spirit of truth and the spirit of falsehood.' It was obviously necessary that Christians, in the age of immediate inspiration, should have some means of discriminating between those who were really under the influence of the Spirit of God and those who were either enthusiasts or deceivers. And the test to which the apostle directed them was rational and easily applied. There were inspired men to whose divine mission and authority God had borne abundant testimony by 'signs, wonders, and various miracles, and gifts of the Holy Spirit' (Hebrews 2:4). As God cannot contradict himself, it follows that anything inconsistent with the teachings of these men, though proceeding from one claiming to be a prophet, must be false and the pretension of its author to inspiration unfounded. Accordingly (1 Corinthians 14:29), the apostle directed that while one prophet spoke, the others were to judge — that is, decide whether he spoke according to the analogy of faith, and whether his inspiration was real, imaginary, or feigned."[186]

---

[186] Charles Hodge, <u>Romans</u>, Romans 12:6.

We must remember that God does speak to His people in the present day; not through *fallible prophets,* but through His living and active word. For the believer, this word is not seen as foolishness, but it is embraced as God's genuine wisdom through the indwelling work of the Holy Spirit. This principle of *Sola Scriptura* does not make the modern church inferior to past ages, nor does it make us fearful of the Holy Spirit. Rather, it makes us utterly dependent upon the Spirit in order to prize, cherish, comprehend, and apply the Scriptures; and in all of this, the believer is abundantly endowed with riches that are eternal and beyond measure. In the parable of the rich man and Lazarus, a final appeal was made by the rich man as he suffered torment in Hades:

Luke 16:27–28: 27 "And he said, 'Then I beg you, father, that you send him to my father's house— 28 for I have five brothers—in order that he may warn them, so that they will not also come to this place of torment.'

This appeal is then addressed in the following exchange:

Luke 16:29–31: 29 "But Abraham said, 'They have Moses and the Prophets; let them hear them.' 30 "But he said, 'No, father Abraham, but if someone goes to them from the dead, they will repent!' 31 "But he said to him, 'If they do not listen to Moses and the Prophets, they will not be persuaded even if someone rises from the dead.' "

Signs, wonders, and great miracles all serve their purpose within the plan of God, seeing that they point us to the glory of God as revealed in His written word. Thus, miracles supply no substitute for God's Holy Writ. This is why the body of Christ is called to desire earnestly God's prophetic revelation, which is now fully revealed in His completed canon of Scripture. This canon of Holy Writ is devoid of human error and corruption; it is perfect, restoring the soul; it is sure, making wise the simple; it is right, rejoicing the heart; it is pure, enlightening the eyes; it is clean, enduring forever; the judgments of the Lord are true, they are righteous altogether; they are more desirable than gold, yes, than much fine gold; sweeter also than honey and the drippings of the honeycomb (Psalm 19:7-10). And what God has revealed will not return to Him empty without accomplishing what He desires (Isaiah 55:11), despite human fallibility, contrivances, or interference.

Finally, in reflection upon all that has been presented in this book, I wish to issue a final word of warning. As mentioned earlier, by relabeling and redefining prophecy, *fallible prophecy* has effectively relabeled and redefined *false prophecy*. The danger that this poses to the church is quite grave, though readily underestimated. When *errorists* are allowed to labor, presumptuously, beneath the label of *prophet*, then the church's necessary guard is dangerously let down. We have already considered the Lord's warning concerning false prophets:

> **Matthew 7:15:** "Beware of the false prophets, who come to you in sheep's clothing, but inwardly are ravenous wolves."

> **Matthew 24:24:** "For false Christs and false prophets will arise and will show great signs and wonders, so as to mislead, if possible, even the elect."

> **Matthew 24:11:** "Many false prophets will arise and will mislead many."

From these texts we see that Christ teaches His disciples three important lessons concerning false prophets: 1. They come by means of stealth, beneath the appearance and presumption of legitimacy (Matthew 7:15); 2. They can even come with many signs and wonders so as to mislead others (Matthew 24:24); and 3. In the last days[187] there will be *many* false

---

[187] By citing Matthew 24 I should note that some who hold to the Dispensational Pre-tribulational view of the rapture would see Christ's warnings as not applying to the church age, but applying to believers in the tribulation period only. The length and breadth of this debate well exceeds the focus of our study, however, I would side with those who see (at

prophets who will mislead *many* (Matthew 24:11). Even in the 1st century church, John warned his readers that *many false prophets* have gone out into the world. In any age, these warnings hold valuable insights for the people of God. Should Christ's church be lured away from the requisite tests of prophecy, she will be exposed to untold dangers. J.C. Ryle is right when he says:

> "Let us beware of the very small beginnings of false doctrine. Every heresy began at one time with some little departure from the truth. There is only a little seed of error needed to create a great tree...It is the omission or addition of one little item in the doctor's prescription that spoils the whole medicine, and turns it into poison...let us never allow a little false doctrine to ruin us, by thinking it is but a 'little one,' and can do no harm."[188]

Even the slightest redaction of God's prescribed tests for prophecy would prove to be potentially fatal should we accept the "little seed" of *fallible prophecy*. Moreover, such a "little seed" bears the potential for personal deception among those who have developed a disproportionate focus on spiritual gifts above the gift Giver Himself: "Many will say to me on that day, 'Lord, Lord, did we not prophesy in Your name...' then I will declare to them, 'I never knew you'" (Matthew 7:15-23). The spiritual danger of presumption, within either the individual or the church, is remarkably grave. The Lord has warned his people about the dangers of those who enter the assembly and falsely *presume* to be prophets (Deuteronomy 18:20-22, Matthew 7:22-23). As well, false prophets and their false prophecies have the capacity *to seduce others from the way in which the Lord commended,* and toleration of such error constitutes a grave danger for those within the assembly of God's people (Deuteronomy 13:1-5). In the end, God's prescribed tests for prophecy call upon the church to flee

---

the very least) Christ's warnings in Matthew 24 as supplying needful instructions to believers in any age and of any eschatological persuasion.

[188] J.C. Ryle, <u>Warnings to the Churches</u>, (Edinburgh, GB: Banner of Truth Trust, 1992), 60-61.

error by pursuing the God of truth, in love, *with all of our heart and all our soul* (Deuteronomy 13:1-5, 1 Corinthians 13, 16:22).

In all of this, I offer this appeal in Christ to the advocates of *fallible prophecy*, whether they might be teachers or students of the doctrine: please reconsider this doctrine of *fallible prophecy* in light of what has been surveyed within the pages of this book. The theology of *fallible prophecy* may appear to be founded upon sound exegesis, but it is not. As well, though popular evangelicals may support such teaching, one must never base his hope and faith upon the popularity of mere men. Grudem's systematic theology continues to spread in its popularity and use in churches and seminaries across the globe, yet we must remember that truth is never ratified by that which is counted as popular among men. In the end, the task of a true shepherd is *not* to direct people to what God *may have said* or what He is *trying to say*, but to direct them to what He *has indeed said*.

Dear reader, God has indeed spoken, and His word will not return to Him empty *without succeeding* in the matter for which He sent it.

Soli Deo Gloria

INDEX

INDEX

INDEX

THE FALLIBLE PROPHETS
OF NEW CALVINISM

By Michael John Beasley

Other titles by this author:

1. All Nations Under God: The Doctrine of Christ's Victorious Atonement - Defined, Defended, and Applied [ISBN: 978-1-935358-03-9].

2. The First Institution: A Theological and Practical Guide for the Reformation of God's Institution of Marriage and Family [ISBN: 978-1-935358-00-8].

3. Indeed, has Paul Really Said?: A Critique of N.T. Wright's Teaching on Justification [ISBN: 978-1-935358-02-2].

4. Altar to an Unknown Love: Rob Bell, C.S. Lewis, and the Legacy of the Art and Thought of Man [ISBN: 978-1-935358-08-4].

published by

The
Armoury
Ministries
www.thearmouryministries.org

Proverbs 3:5-18:

5 Trust in Jehovah with all thy heart,
And lean not upon thine own understanding:
6 In all thy ways acknowledge him, And he will direct thy paths.
7 Be not wise in thine own eyes; Fear Jehovah, and depart from
evil: 8 It will be health to thy navel, And marrow to thy bones. 9
Honor Jehovah with thy substance, And with the first-fruits of
all thine increase: 10 So shall thy barns be filled with plenty, And
thy vats shall overflow with new wine. 11 My son, despise not
the chastening of Jehovah; Neither be weary of his reproof: 12
For whom Jehovah loveth he reproveth; Even as a father the son
in whom he delighteth. 13 Happy is the man that findeth
wisdom, And the man that getteth understanding. 14 For the
gaining of it is better than the gaining of silver, And the profit
thereof than fine gold. 15 She is more precious than rubies: And
none of the things thou canst desire are to be compared unto
her. 16 Length of days is in her right hand; In her left hand are
riches and honor. 17 Her ways are ways
of pleasantness, And all her
paths are peace.
18 She is a
tree of life
to them that
lay hold
upon her:
And happy
is every
one that
retaineth
her.

CPSIA information can be obtained
at www.ICGtesting.com
Printed in the USA
FSOW01n1055061014
3189FS